THE TOTAL CARTOONIST

THE TOTAL CARTOONIST

BY KEN MUSE
AND
PRENTICE-HALL, INC.
ENGLEWOOD CLIFFS, N.J. 07632

Library of Congress Cataloging in Publication Data

Muse, Ken   (date)
   The total cartoonist.

   Includes index.
   1. Cartooning.   I. Title.
NC1320.M87 1984   741.5   83-3354
ISBN   0-13-925263-0

Editorial/production supervision: **Karen Skrable**
Interior design: **Ken Muse**
Cover design: **Ken Muse**
Manufacturing buyer: **Anthony Caruso**

Printed in the United States of America

10   9   8   7   6   5   4   3   2

ISBN 0-13-925263-0

PRENTICE-HALL INTERNATIONAL, INC., *London*
PRENTICE-HALL OF AUSTRALIA PTY. LIMITED, *Sydney*
EDITORA PRENTICE-HALL DO BRASIL, LTDA., *Rio de Janeiro*
PRENTICE-HALL CANADA INC., *Toronto*
PRENTICE-HALL OF INDIA PRIVATE LIMITED, *New Delhi*
PRENTICE-HALL OF JAPAN, INC., *Tokyo*
PRENTICE-HALL OF SOUTHEAST ASIA PTE. LTD., *Singapore*
WHITEHALL BOOKS LIMITED, *Wellington, New Zealand*

BAD ART IS BAD ART
AND ALL THE
MONEY AND FAME
IN THE WORLD
ISN'T GOING
TO CHANGE IT!

KEN MUSE...THAT'S ME. BEEN ACTIVELY INVOLVED IN ART AND PHOTOGRAPHY SINCE AS FAR BACK AS I CAN RECALL! DID A COMIC STRIP FOR McNAUGHT BACK IN THE 60'S CALLED "WAYOUT." BEEN IN TELEVISION, ANIMATION, TECH ILLUSTRATION, ADVERTISING, PHOTOGRAPHY, AND WRITING BOOKS.... ALSO TEACHING COMMERCIAL ART, PHOTO-GRAPHY & CARTOONING FOR MACOMB COMMUNITY COLLEGE IN WARREN, MICHIGAN FOR 15 YEARS. THIS IS MY FOURTH BOOK FOR PRENTICE-HALL! THE SECOND ONE ON THE ART OF CARTOONING. IT'S BEEN GREAT FUN, *HOPE YOU LIKE IT.*

THE BiG BAD TABLE of CONTENTS

THE BiG BAD TABLE of CONTENTS

THE BIG BAD TABLE of CONTENTS

THE BIG BAD TABLE OF CONTENTS

CARTOONISTS' MOTTO: GOOD IDEAS-GOOD ART

CREATING

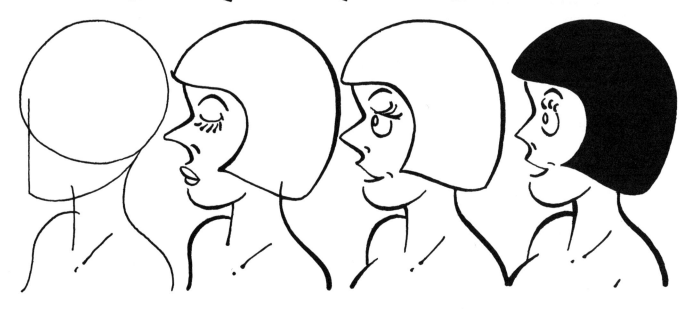

A CHARACTER!

PROBABLY THE MOST DIFFICULT
THING TO DO, AND JUST AS
DIFFICULT TO EXPLAIN, IS HOW
A CARTOON CHARACTER IS
DEVELOPED BY THE CARTOONIST.
THE PROCESS CAN INVOLVE
MANY HOURS AT THE DRAWING
BOARD.... EVEN WEEKS AND
MONTHS BEFORE YOU ARE
SATISFIED. AND EVEN THEN IT
MIGHT BE A DEAD END. IN MANY
CASES THE CHARACTER YOU
HAVE SO CAREFULLY WORKED
TO PERFECTION KEEPS ON
CHANGING INTO SOMETHING
OTHER THAN INTENDED IF YOU
GET SLOPPY AND PAY LESS
ATTENTION TO YOUR WORK.

EVERY PROFESSIONAL CARTOONIST
KNOWS OVER A LONG PERIOD OF
TIME, HIS CAREFULLY DRAWN
CHARACTER WILL CHANGE VERY
GRADUALLY IN SUBTLE WAYS.
THESE CHANGES COME ABOUT
THROUGH REFINEMENTS IN
DRAWING TECHNIQUE AND IN
INKING. IF THERE ARE ANY
CHORES IN CARTOONING, THIS
IS THE TOUGHEST:

TO HOLD THE CHARACTER

THE PROFESSIONAL HOLDS THE
CHARACTER SURPRISINGLY WELL.
IF YOU LOOK BACK AT THE FIRST
"PEANUTS" STRIP, YOU'LL FIND THE
HEADS A LITTLE ROUNDER THAN
THEY ARE NOW- BUT NOT THAT
MUCH. A TERRIFIC IMPROVEMENT
HAS TAKEN PLACE.
ANOTHER REMARKABLE CHANGE
AND IMPROVEMENT OVER THE
YEARS IS "DICK TRACY."

EVEN THOUGH THE CARTOONIST
KNOWS THIS CHANGE IN THE
CHARACTER DRAWING HAS TO
HAPPEN, EVERY DRAWING IS
WORKED HARD TO HOLD THE
CHARACTER. I MENTIONED
HOW INKING IS A FACTOR
IN THE SUBTLE CHANGE OF A
CHARACTER. REMEMBER....
WHEN AN ARTIST INKS, THE
BRISTOL IS **TURNED.** THIS
TURNING OF THE BRISTOL
DURING INKING HAS AN EFFECT
ON THE PRESSURE AND LINE
VARIATION. MOST PROFESSIONALS
TURN THE BRISTOL TO PRODUCE
THE EASIEST INKING POSITION.
THAT IS TO SAY, IT'S EASIER FOR
SOME CARTOONISTS TO INK IN
CERTAIN DIRECTIONS, AND MORE
DIFFICULT IN OTHERS.
THEREFORE, IF YOU GRADUALLY
CHANGE DIRECTION INKING, YOU'LL
CHANGE THE CHARACTER.

LET'S CREATE A COMIC STRIP

CREATING A NEW COMIC STRIP IS EASIER IF YOU HAVE SOME GOAL IN MIND...THAT IS IF YOU KNOW EXACTLY WHAT KIND OF CHARACTER YOU WANT, AND THE TYPE OF HUMOR THAT'S EASY FOR YOU. YOUR STRIP SHOULD BE ABOUT SITUATIONS THAT ARE FAMILIAR TO YOU SO YOU WON'T READILY RUN OUT OF IDEAS. FOR EXAMPLE, LET'S DECIDE ON A STUPID SORT OF GUY, ON THE SHY SIDE, AND REALLY NAÏVE. A GOOD PLACE TO START WOULD BE HIS **FACE.** SO...THE NEXT PAGE WILL START A STEP-BY-STEP DEMONSTRATION!

IT IS CERTAINLY NO EASY TASK DEVELOPING A CHARACTER FOR A NEW COMIC STRIP OR PANEL. RIGHT AWAY YOU'RE FACED WITH A BUNCH OF DECISIONS YOU NEVER DREAMED EXISTED!

YEH, LIKE HOW WILL THE CHARACTER LOOK...HOW MANY HEADS TALL... WHAT KIND OF PERSONALITY... WHAT TYPE OF CAREER OR SOCIAL GROUP... WHAT KIND OF PEN POINT FOR DRAWING... WHAT TYPE OF PEN FOR LETTERING... WHAT KIND OF BALLOONS... WHAT TYPE OF HUMOR, AND WHAT SIZE SHALL I DRAW?

YOU COULD JUST DRAW A FUNNY LOOKING CHARACTER AND LET IT DEVELOP! I DON'T RECOMMEND DOING THIS!

6

IT STARTS WITH A FUNNY GUY, FOUR HEADS TALL WITH A BIG, BIG NOSE! THE NOSE CHANGES THE MOST IN CARTOONS.

SEE?...THE NOSE IS GETTING SMALLER AND THE GUY HAS SHRUNK TO 4½ HEADS! PANT LEGS ARE WIDENING.

THE CHANGE IS STARK! HE GOT WIDER IN THE BODY AND FEET! A MUCH FUNNIER CARTOON.

IF YOU START WITH A CHARACTER THAT YOU JUST HAVEN'T GIVEN MUCH THOUGHT, AND START DRAWING THE COMIC STRIP, YOU'RE ASKING FOR TROUBLE. LIKE ABOVE, OVER A PERIOD OF TIME, THERE WILL BE SUBTLE CHANGES, RESULTING IN A GRADUAL REFINEMENT. THE FIRST WEEK OF STRIPS WILL LOOK DIFFERENT THAN THE FIFTH WEEK!

WHAT HAPPENS THEN? YOU'LL HAVE TO REDRAW ALL THE ORIGINAL STRIPS............CHANGING THE CHARACTER TO LOOK LIKE YOUR CURRENT ONE. YOU'LL REDRAW THEM FOR THE GAGS. DO YOU REALIZE THE FRUSTRATION REDRAWING WEEKS OF COMIC STRIPS?

MY ADVICE IS TO PLAN THE CHARACTER...TAKE TIME, DECIDE, AND THEN PUT IT ON TRACING PAPER WHERE YOU CAN REFER TO IT... AND *RETRACE IT!*

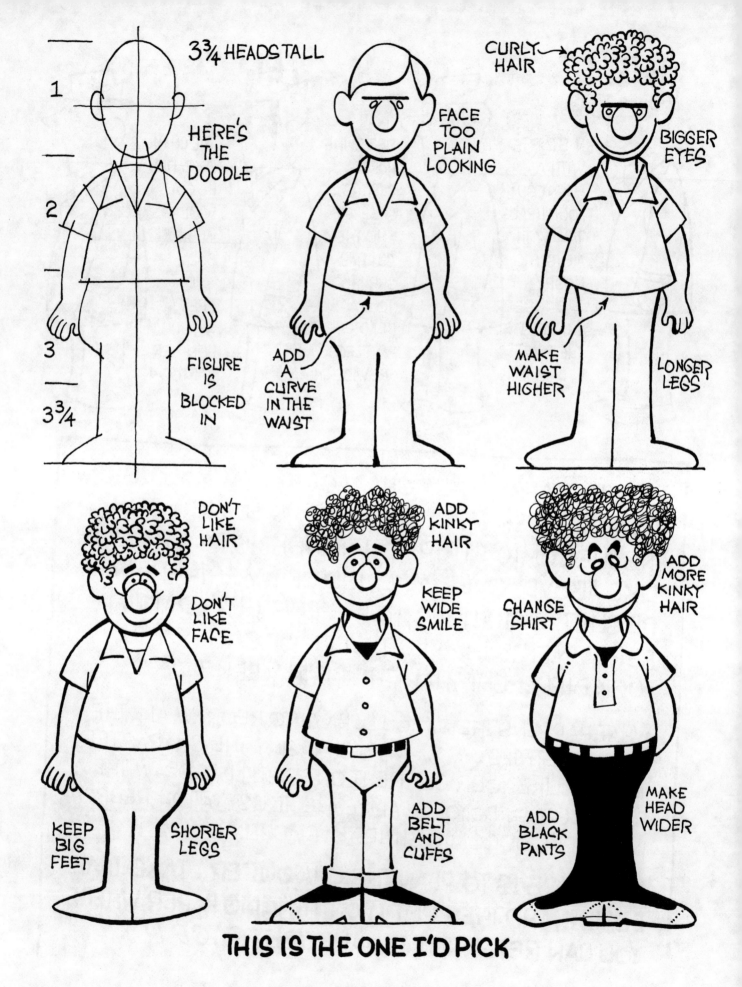

3¾ HEADS TALL

1

2

3

3¾

HERE'S THE DOODLE

FIGURE IS BLOCKED IN

FACE TOO PLAIN LOOKING

ADD A CURVE IN THE WAIST

CURLY HAIR

BIGGER EYES

MAKE WAIST HIGHER

LONGER LEGS

DON'T LIKE HAIR

DON'T LIKE FACE

KEEP BIG FEET

SHORTER LEGS

ADD KINKY HAIR

KEEP WIDE SMILE

ADD BELT AND CUFFS

CHANGE SHIRT

ADD MORE KINKY HAIR

ADD BLACK PANTS

MAKE HEAD WIDER

THIS IS THE ONE I'D PICK

8

THE SUBTLE CHARACTER CHANGES
FROM INKING!

LINE VARIATION IS AT THE TOP OF NOSE

NOTE THE LINE VARIATION HERE

LINE VARIATION NOW AT BOTTOM

IT BEGINS WITH A WELL PLANNED CHARACTER

THEN THE NOSE GROWS AND THE BACK OF THE HEAD GETS POINTIER

THE NOSE IS STILL GROWING, THE HEAD IS POINTIER, AND THE HAIR IS CHANGING.

HAT IS HIGHER

HAIR IS DIFFERENT

BACK OF HEAD IS POINTED

BACK IS MORE ROUNDED

NOSE AND EYES ARE BIGGER

NOW, BY COMPARING THE FIRST WELL INTENTIONED INKED CHARACTER WITH THE LAST ONE, YOU CAN CERTAINLY SEE THE DIFFERENCE. NOTICE ALSO THE MOUTH IS SLIGHTLY LOWER TO THE CHIN.

THESE CHANGES DON'T COME ABOUT BY CHANGING PEN POINTS, THEY COME ABOUT THROUGH THE CHANGE THE CARTOONIST FEELS ABOUT HIS CHARACTER...AND GAGS.

THE VERY FIRST THING IN CREATING YOUR CHARACTER, IS DRAWING SOMEONE THAT YOU CAN LIVE WITH.....SOMEONE YOU ARE GOING TO ENJOY DRAWING...DAY AFTER DAY!

THE FIRST RULE

AVOID SHAPES YOU'RE GOING TO HAVE DIFFICULTY INKING.

THE BACK OF THIS HEAD MAY BE TOO DIFFICULT FOR YOU TO INK AND KEEP THE LINE EVEN. YOU NEED TO INK IN A CONTINOUS FREE FLOWING LINE.

MAKING THE BACK OF THE HEAD FLATTER COULD MAKE IT EASIER TO INK BECAUSE OF DOWN MOTION. THE INKING IS DONE IN TWO SEPERATE MOTIONS.

EVEN THOUGH THE INKING MOTIONS ARE EASIER IN THIS ONE, THE CHARACTER FEELING IS LOST. NOTICE WHAT THE LINE VARIATION DOES FOR THE ART?

INK IN THE DIRECTION THAT IS *EASIEST* FOR YOU

LET'S BEGIN WITH THE FACE !

YOU COULD BEGIN BY DRAWING PAGES FULL OF FUNNY FACES TO WARM-UP AND GET IN THE MOOD. THIS COULD BE A GOOD WAY TO START, ESPECIALLY IF YOU DON'T HAVE ANY PARTICULAR IDEA IN MIND. THE BIG THING ABOUT THIS METHOD IS YOU'RE *NOT RESTRICTED !*

SO... AFTER PAGES AND PAGES OF FACES, THIS ONE LOOKS LIKE IT HAS POSSIBILITIES, BUT IT NEEDS SOME DEVELOPING. ONE OF THE SECRETS IS TO MAKE IT *FUNNIER!*
SO LET'S *MAKE* IT FUNNIER.

WE CAN START BY MAKING THE NOSE SMALLER, BUT THE HEAD IS TOO BOTTOM-WEIGHTED, AND THE MOUTH IS OUT OF PLACE AND TOO WIDE.

THIS CHANGE TO AN EGG-SHAPED HEAD MAKES THE HEAD MORE BALANCED... AND WITH A SMALLER MOUTH, IT'S BEGINNING TO LOOK FUNNIER.

MORE HAIR, SMALLER AND HIGHER MOUTH.... PLUS A HEAVY LINE AROUND HAIR FOR BACKGROUND SEPARATION.

I CAN'T GO ALONG WITH THIS ONE. THE THIN BODY MAKES HIM LOOK LIKE A YOUNG STUDENT. THE HEAD SEEMS OUT OF PLACE, AND I'M NOT GETTING THAT STUPID LOOK. MAYBE HE'S DRESSED WRONG, OR MAYBE HE'S NOT WALKING THE RIGHT WAY TO GIVE THE FEELING OF BEING SHY.... THE WHOLE THING IS NOT RIGHT!

GILLOTTS 170

I ALWAYS TRY THE FAT APPROACH WITH ALL MY NEW CHARACTERS. THIS ONE IS NOT WORKING EITHER. I'M STILL NOT GETTING THAT STUPID LOOK, AND HE DOESN'T LOOK AWKWARD ENOUGH... AND CERTAINLY NOT SHY!

GILLOTTS 290

I DID IT! I ADDED A SILLY HAT, BIG FEET, WEARING GOLF SHOES, A BENT-OVER LOOK, AND BOTH ARMS IN THE SAME POSITION... AND HE REALLY DOESN'T LOOK LIKE HE'S **ALL THERE.** TERRIFIC... THAT'S JUST WHAT I WANT. LET'S GIVE HIM SOME RIDICULOUS NAME, LIKE: **SUPER SILLY WILLIE.**

GILLOTTS 1290

SO NOW THAT WE'VE ESTABLISHED HOW OUR CHARACTER LOOKS, HIS NAME, HOW HE DRESSES, AND HOW HE WALKS... WE'LL TAKE THE NEXT STEP AND GET TOGETHER A MONTH OF STRIPS... (THAT'S 24), WITH SOME GOOD GAGS. THEY ALL HAVE TO BE FUNNY. THROW OUT THE WEAK ONES.

REMEMBER... THE GAGS HAVE TO FIT THE TYPE OF PERSON WILLIE IS: SHY, AWKWARD, NAÏVE, AND NOT TOO SWIFT... SO GET YOURSELF SOME BOND PAPER AND LET'S GET STARTED!

IT MIGHT BE HELPFUL IF WE GAVE HIM AN OCCUPATION OF SORTS. THAT SHOULD HELP WITH SOME OF THE GAGS. LET'S MAKE HIM A CHEMIST!

SO NOW WILLIE HAS A BOSS AND CO-WORKERS, AND SOME SITUATIONS WE CAN USE TO CREATE GAGS. YOU WON'T NEED TO BE A CHEMIST TO WRITE GAGS FOR A STRIP LIKE THIS.. JUST SITUATIONS!

LET'S START WITH A COMMON SITUATION, WHERE OUR CHARACTER, WILLIE, IS IN HIS **BOSS'S** OFFICE AT THE DINOSAUR CHEMICAL COMPANY.

IN THIS SITUATION, HIS BOSS, MR. ZOOUCKY, IS CONCERNED ABOUT WILLIE'S CO-WORKERS NOT TAKING HIM SERIOUSLY. THIS IS A **NATURAL** FOR A GAG!

I'VE ALWAYS HAD SUCCESS WITH JUST STARTING OUT WITHOUT ANY GAG IN MIND... SO THE FIRST PANEL WAS DRAWN WITH THIS LEAD-IN COMMENT.

© KEN MUSE

THE GAG DIDN'T COME TO ME UNTIL I ADDED THE SECOND PANEL. IT SEEMED LIKE A NATURAL FOR WILLIE TO DO WHAT HE DID. *REMEMBER......IN HUMOR......* ONE OF THE KEY ELEMENTS IS SURPRISE. **THE UNEXPECTED!**

WE NOW KNOW WHAT KIND OF A GUY WILLIE IS! A GOOD NUMBER OF THE GAGS CAN BE BUILT ON THIS TYPE OF PERSON. *LET'S RUN A PAGE OF WILLIE, AND SEE!*

A SECTION OF THE STRIP IN ORIGINAL SIZE!

© KEN MUSE

AS YOU CAN SEE, I DON'T SPEND A LOT OF TIME ON
MY GAG ROUGHS. THEY'RE FAST AND QUICK. JUST
ENOUGH SO THAT I KNOW WHAT'S GOING ON.
I'D RATHER SPEND THE TIME ON THE FINISHED COMIC STRIP!

ORIGINAL SIZE

BOTH OF THESE STRIPS START WITH NORMAL CONVERSATION AND PROGRESS INTO A SURPRISE. *YOU COULD WORK BACKWARDS!*

THEN, AS I WAS ABOUT TO REMEMBER WHAT I FORGOT, I REMEMBER FORGETTING WHAT I FORGOT TO REMEMBER....

...THEN I FORGOT!

ORIGINAL SIZE

© KEN MUSE

I FORGOT MY AMNESIA, AND DIDN'T REMEMBER WHAT I FORGOT TO FORGET!

THEN, AS I WAS ABOUT TO REMEMBER WHAT I FORGOT, I REMEMBER FORGETTING WHAT I FORGOT TO REMEMBER....

...THEN I FORGOT!

ONE THING ABOUT GAGS, ESPECIALLY IF YOU DEVOTE A LOT OF TIME TRYING TO DEVELOP THEM, IS THEY START OFF WITH NORMAL CONVERSATION, OR ACTION...THAT IS REALLY THE KEY, BECAUSE IF THEY DIDN'T, THERE WOULD BE NO SURPRISE. THE SURPRISE IS FROM THE DEVIATION FROM THE NORMAL SEQUENCE OF DIALOG, WHICH YOU EXPECT, BUT DON'T GET...*THAT'S FUNNY!*

EXAGGERATION!

NOTICE HOW THE LINE VARIATION CHANGES?

BEGINNING WITH A TYPICAL CARTOON CHARACTER FOR A BASIS OF EXAGGERATION, WE PROGRESS TO THE SECOND DRAWING. THE WALK IS MADE FUNNIER BY STIFFER LEGS, A WIDER SWING TO THE ARMS AND A STUPID FACE WITH A BIG NOSE. IN DRAWING THREE, THE BODY GETS LONGER, THE LEGS GET SHORTER AND FATTER AND THE HEAD AND NOSE GET BIGGER!

I DID THESE EXAMPLES WITH THE AID OF TRACING PAPER — WHAT WOULD WE DO WITHOUT IT? YOU CAN CARRY EXAGGERATION TOO FAR—TOTALLY DESTROYING YOUR ORIGINAL IDEA! WHEN YOU ARRIVE AT SOMETHING FUNNY.... STOP.!!!

MORE EXAGGERATION!

NOTICE AGAIN HOW THE LINE VARIATION ENHANCES THE COMIC APPEARANCE . . . .

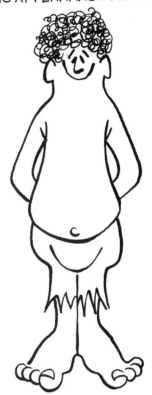

THE SECOND DRAWING IS FUNNIER THAN THE FIRST, BUT THE EXAGGERATION HAS GONE TOO FAR IN THE THIRD DRAWING – DESTROYING THE ORIGINAL CONCEPT.

THE THIRD ONE IS THE FUNNIEST, BUT THE FOURTH ONE IS JUST SILLY!

EXAGGERATION CAN ALSO GO TOO FAR IN "FACES."

FIGURE ONE

FIGURE TWO

FIGURE THREE

FIGURE ONE IS REALLY THE BEST CHARACTER BECAUSE IT IS THE SIMPLEST! FIGURE TWO IS ONE STEP FURTHER IN EXAGGERATION BUT HAS LOST THE ORIGINAL FEELING. IT IS A FAILURE BECAUSE *EVERYTHING* HAS BEEN EXAGGERATED, ... AND THAT'S *NOT* THE SECRET! FIGURE THREE HAS BEEN TONED-DOWN WITH CLOTHES INTO A GOOD CHARACTER—BUT NOT AS GOOD AS THE ORIGINAL!

INKING ENHANCEMENT

INKING THE CARTOON IS AS MUCH FUN AS DRAWING THE CARTOON. INKING CHANGES THE CHARACTER. A PENCIL DRAWING LOOKS DIFFERENT THAN AN INK DRAWING BECAUSE THE APPLICATION IS DIFFERENT. INK IS HARD COLD LINES... PENCIL IS SOFT, TONED, AND HAS SUBTLE LINE VARIATION!

BUT YOU CAN KILL A CARTOON CREATION BY INKING. YOU CAN NEVER SEEM TO DUPLICATE THAT PENCIL CREATION INTO AN INK DRAWING, NO MATTER HOW HARD YOU TRY!

YES, BUT IF YOU WORK AT IT, YOU CAN COME CLOSE... AND SOMETIMES DO A *BETTER* JOB THAN THE PENCIL... BUT IT TAKES PRACTICE.

INKING WITH A MAGIC MARKER IS A *BUMMER*! THERE'S ABOUT AS MUCH LIFE IN A MAGIC MARKER AS A *COTTON SWAB*!

CHANGES THROUGH INKING

WHEN IT COMES TO INKING, LINE VARIATION IS THE NAME OF THE GAME. IT'S THAT ONE SINGLE THING THAT GIVES YOUR CARTOON **CLASS.**

MORE CHANGES
CREATED BY INKING!

GILLOTTS 1290, ALL OF THIS PAGE

NOTICE THE EFFECT OF PEN PRESSURE?

SOME INKING TECHNIQUES TO TRY

GILLOTTS 1290
VERY SLIGHT VARIATION
WITH ALL LINES TOUCHING

GILLOTTS 1290
HEAVY LINE VARIATION
WITH ALL LINES TOUCHING

GILLOTTS 1290
VERY HEAVY VARIATION
WITH ALL LINES TOUCHING

HUNT 102 QUILL
OUTLINED WITH AN B5½
HUNT SPEEDBALL

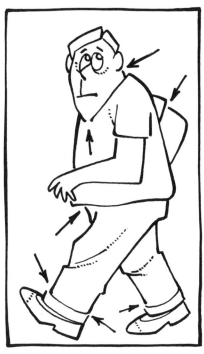

GILLOTTS 1290
MEDIUM LINE VARIATION,
NOT ALL LINES TOUCHING

NO. 1 BRUSH
A BRUSH MAKES ALL
THE LINES STAND OUT

INKING TECHNIQUES

GILLOTTS 170
LINE VARIATION BETWEEN
GILLOTTS 1290 AND 290

GILLOTTS 170
THIS IS A GREAT PEN
FOR A SHAGLINE

SPEEDBALL B6
NICE EVEN LINES FOR
THAT DESIGN LOOK

GILLOTTS 1066
THIN SHARP LINES WITH
SOME SHADED AREAS

GILLOTTS 290
A WELL THOUGHT OUT
LINE VARIATION

HUNT 513
FAST AND SLOPPY
FREE MOVING LINES

INKING TECHNIQUES

NO.4 BRUSH
BOLDER BRUSH STROKES
REALLY DRAW ATTENTION

GILLOTTS 1290
INTERESTING DOTTED
EFFECT. UNUSUAL STYLE.

GILLOTTS 290
DOTS AND PATTERNS THAT
FOLLOW THE CONTOURS

GILLOTTS 290
ADDING MORE BLACKS
AND ONLY ONE PATTERN

GILLOTTS 1290 WITH LINES
NOT TOUCHING, SOME ARE
DOTTED..AND SOME BLACKS

GILLOTTS 1290
CLEAN LINES AND SOME
SOLID BLACKS FOR DESIGN

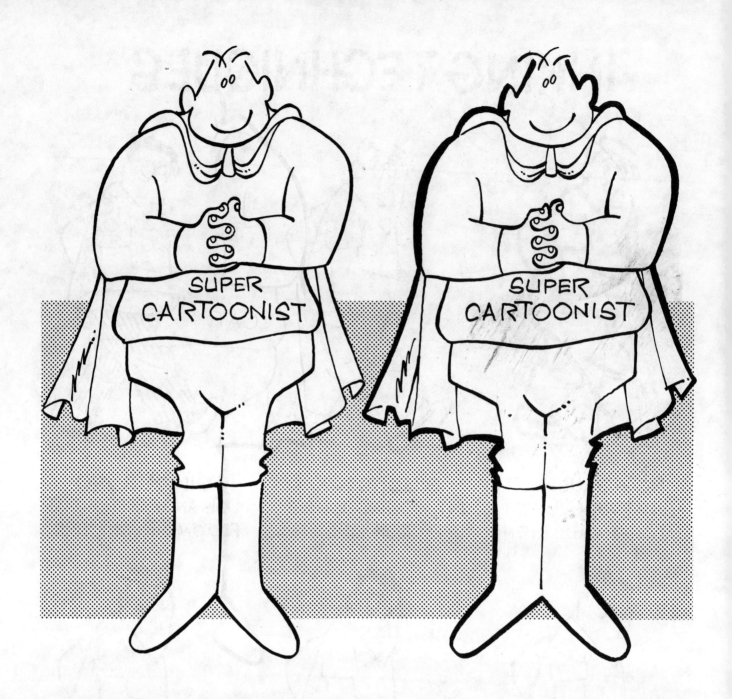

HERE'S AN INKING TECHNIQUE THAT DOES WONDERS FOR YOUR CARTOONS—EVEN THE BADLY DRAWN ONES—YOU SIMPLY ADD A THICK LINE AROUND THE WHOLE CARTOON—BEFORE YOU INK IT. IF YOU INK IT FIRST IT WON'T HAVE THAT "LOOSE FEELING".... A GILLOTT 1290 PEN POINT WAS USED FOR THE OUTLINE AND THE DRAWING. A SPEEDBALL WILL DO THE SAME FOR THE HEAVY OUTLINE BUT IS TOO *MECHANICAL!* IT LOOKS BETTER IF THE OUTLINE HAS A LITTLE LINE VARIATION—*TRY IT.....*

NOTICE THE DIFFERENCE IN THESE TWO? THERE'S NOT ENOUGH LINE VARIATION IN THE SECOND ONE TO STAND UP TO THE HEAVY OUTLINE. THE CONTRAST IN LINE IS TOO GREAT... IT'S JUST A GIMMICK. THE HEAVY OUTLINE IS A SPEEDBALL B5, AND THE INKING IS A GILLOTT 170! TRY THIS EXPERIMENT ON ONE OF YOUR CARTOONS & SEE WHAT IT DOES TO YOUR STYLE — GREAT FUN!

HERE'S A PANEL FROM ONE OF MY COMIC STRIPS, INKED WITH A GILLOTT 1290 – AND NO HEAVY OUTLINE. NICE BUT NOT OUTSTANDING!

HERE'S A PANEL FROM ONE OF MY COMIC STRIPS. INKED WITH A GILLOTT 1290 – AND NO HEAVY OUTLINE. NICE BUT NOT OUTSTANDING!

43% REDUCTION

SAME PANEL, SAME PEN POINT, ONLY OUTLINED WITH HEAVY PRESSURE. NOTICE THE INTEREST CREATED BY THIS STYLE OF INKING!

SAME PANEL, SAME PEN POINT, ONLY OUTLINED WITH HEAVY PRESSURE. NOTICE THE INTEREST CREATED BY THIS STYLE OF INKING!

43% REDUCTION

HOW INKING SETS THE MOOD

WINSOR & NEWTON #2 BRUSH   HUNT SPEEDBALL A5   GILLOTTS 170

NO.2 BRUSH   HUNT QUILL 202   GILLOTTS 1290   HUNT SPEEDBALL B6

IF YOU WILL NOTICE, THE BRUSH HAS THE GREATEST
EFFECT ON THE CARTOON CHARACTER. THIS IS ALSO
TRUE IN SERIOUS ILLUSTRATION. ALSO NOTICE THE
FLEXIBLE PEN POINT RUNS A CLOSE SECOND!

INKING EXERCISES

GILLOTTS 290   GILLOTTS 170   GILLOTTS 170   GILLOTTS 1290   GILLOTTS 1290

GILLOTTS 290   HUNT 513   GILLOTTS 170   GILLOTTS 1066   GILLOTTS 290

GILLOTTS 1290   GILLOTTS 290   GILLOTTS 404   GILLOTTS 170   HUNT 102

HUNT 102   GILLOTTS 303   GILLOTTS 1066   GILLOTTS 303   HUNT 102

GILLOTTS 303   B5   B5½   FB3   GILLOTTS 1290

INKING EXERCISES...

GILLOTTS 170	GILLOTTS 170	GILLOTTS 170	GILLOTTS 170	GILLOTTS 1290
GILLOTTS 170	GILLOTTS 290	GILLOTTS 290	GILLOTTS 1290	GILLOTTS 1290
GILLOTTS 170	GILLOTTS 290	GILLOTTS 290	GILLOTTS 170	GILLOTTS 1290
NO.1 BRUSH	NO.2 BRUSH	NO.2 BRUSH	NO.1 BRUSH	NO.1 BRUSH
NO.1 BRUSH	NO.1 BRUSH	NO.1 BRUSH	NO.2 BRUSH	NO.2 BRUSH

THERE'S AN OLD RULE OF THUMB THAT'S BEEN AROUND IN THE PROFESSION FOR A LONG TIME. I HAVE NO IDEA WHERE IT ORIGINATED, BUT I'LL PASS IT ALONG TO YOU:

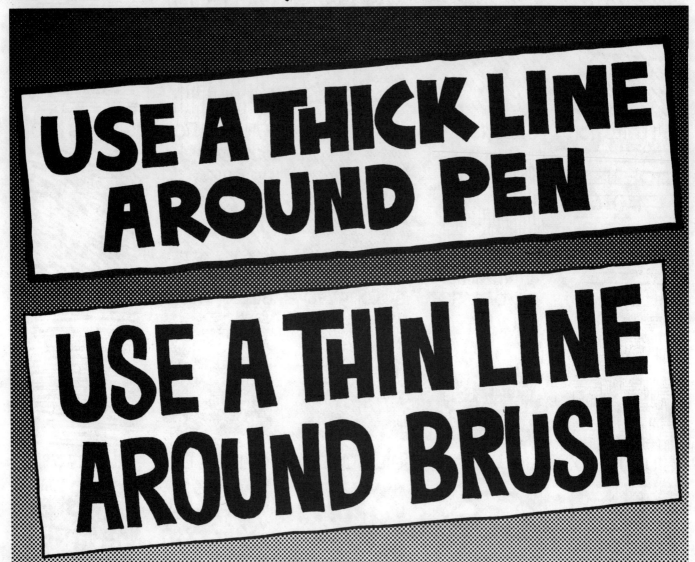

USE A THICK LINE AROUND PEN

USE A THIN LINE AROUND BRUSH

THERE ARE OF COURSE EXCEPTIONS TO THESE RULES. FOR EXAMPLE, IF YOU USED A GILLOTTS 1290 OR 290, WHICH ARE VERY FLEXIBLE, YOU WOULD GET LINES SIMILAR TO A BRUSH. I'VE DRAWN SOME EXAMPLES ON THE NEXT FEW PAGES TO ILLUSTRATE THIS POINT.

IF YOU DON'T EXPERIMENT YOU WON'T SURVIVE!

SWITCHING TO BRUSH

I'LL HAVE A CUP OF COFFEE AND A BOTTLE OF INK, WITH A NO. 3 BRUSH!

IF YOU'VE BEEN INKING YOUR CARTOONS WITH PEN POINTS, THE SWITCH-OVER TO BRUSH WILL BE A BIG DECISION. A BRUSH WILL NOTICEABLY CHANGE THE LOOK AND THE MOOD OF YOUR CARTOONS. THE BRUSH NECESSITATES A SOFTER PRESSURE AND MORE ATTENTION. THE PEN RUNS OUT OF INK QUICKLY, BUT THE BRUSH DOES SO GRADUALLY, CAUSING A DRY BRUSH EFFECT. IT'S AN UNNERVING EXPERIENCE. ALSO, THE POINTS ON YOUR FAVORITE BRUSHES WILL DETERIORATE BECAUSE OF THE DAMAGING EFFECT OF DIPPING THEM IN INK, EATING AWAY AT THE FINE POINTS. YOU WILL BE ALWAYS ON THE LOOKOUT FOR GOOD BRUSHES, BUT IF YOU MASTER THEM YOUR WORK WILL BE BEAUTIFUL. YOU'LL ALSO FIND A MEDIUM SURFACE BRISTOL WILL BE EASIER TO WORK RATHER THAN A PLATE. (HIGH GLOSS)

THIS IS WHAT A BRUSH DOES...

THE LITTLE GUY ON THE LEFT WAS INKED WITH A GILLOTTS 170 PEN. THE OTHER GUY WITH A NO. 2 BRUSH.

THIS ONE IS REVERSED. NOTICE THE BRUSH IS GETTING ALL THE ATTENTION. ANY SIZE BRUSH DOES IT.!

NOTICE HOW EACH CHARACTER CHANGES FROM INKING?

HERE ARE SOME SUGGESTIONS AND POINTERS ON USING A BRUSH

TRY A PLATE AND MEDIUM FINISH BRISTOL, SO YOU CAN DECIDE WHICH IS THE MOST FUN

"POINT" YOUR BRUSH - NOT ON THE NECK OF THE BOTTLE, BUT ON A SCRAP OF BRISTOL, OR PAPER

WORK A LITTLE LARGER THAN YOU WOULD WITH A PEN - IT'S EASIER

KEEP YOUR BRUSHES CLEAN WITH WARM WATER AND A MILD DISH SOAP

GET THE BEST BRUSHES YOU CAN

"WARM-UP" ON SCRAP BRISTOL BEFORE YOU INK YOUR WORK

TRY SEVERAL SIZES - DIFFERENT STROKES FOR DIFFERENT FOLKS!

USE A PEN TO TOUCH-UP THE RAGGED EDGES

STUDY THE WORK OF OTHER CARTOONISTS WHO USE *BRUSHES!*

NO. ONE BRUSH, USING LIGHT PRESSURE TO KEEP THE LINE MORE ON THE THIN SIDE.

YOU MIGHT WANT TO TRY THIS SYSTEM: THIN THE INK WITH DISTILLED WATER. THAT WILL IMPROVE THE FLOW... WHICH MEANS THE INK WILL NOT STAND MUCH ERASURE. THERE ARE TWO WAYS TO HANDLE THIS.

NO. THREE BRUSH, USING BOLD STROKES AND HAVING A GOOD TIME. BE SURE TO USE A SOFT EBERHARD FABER KNEADED PLASTIC RUBBER ERASER... NO. 1224.

FIRST WAY: DRAW LIGHTLY WITH A 6H OR 7H PENCIL... SO YOU WON'T HAVE TO ERASE.

SECOND WAY: USE A NON-REPRO SKY BLUE PENCIL FOR DRAWING. NO. 740½. EVEN IF YOU BRUSH WITH INK THAT IS UNDILUTED, IT WILL STILL **GRAY-UP** WHEN YOU ERASE!

GILLOTTS 170   HUNT SPEEDBALL B6 FOR OUTLINE

MEDIUM LINE AROUND A PEN DRAWING.

THIS IS A TERRIFIC COMPROMISE FOR PEN DRAWING. THERE'S A NICE BALANCE HERE THAT ADDS TO THE WHOLE FEELING. YOU'LL FIND THAT A FREEHAND LINE LOOKS BETTER.

WINSOR-NEWTON SERIES 7 NO.2 BRUSH

MEDIUM LINE AROUND A BRUSH DRAWING.

ANOTHER GOOD COMPROMISE THAT DOESN'T TAKE AWAY FROM THE BRUSH WORK, BUT STILL HOLDS THE *WHOLE THING* TOGETHER! THIS WOULD BE A GREAT CHOICE, AND LOOKS PRO.

WINSOR-NEWTON NO.2 BRUSH   HUNT QUILL 202 FOR OUTLINE

VERY THIN LINE AROUND A BRUSH DRAWING. THE IDEA IS THAT THE THIN LINE IS SUPPOSED TO ACCENT THE BRUSH LINES. MOST COMIC BOOKS ARE INKED IN BRUSH... AND YOU'LL NOTICE THE THIN LINES AROUND THE ART.

WINSOR-NEWTON NO.2 BRUSH   SPEEDBALL FB3 FOR OUTLINE

VERY THICK LINE AROUND A BRUSH DRAWING. THE THEORY ON THIS ONE IS THE HEAVY OUTLINE OVERPOWERS THE BRUSH LINES. COMPARED TO THE TOP SQUARE, IT DOES. IT'S TOO OVERPOWERING! STRIP ARTISTS GO FOR THE THICKIES.

42

GILLOTTS 170   HUNT QUILL 202 FOR OUTLINE

VERY THIN LINE AROUND A PEN DRAWING.
THIS APPROACH DOES NOT GIVE ENOUGH CONTRAST TO THE PEN LINES. HOWEVER, THIS WOULD DEPEND ON HOW YOU USED PRESSURE ON YOUR PEN POINT. IT'S ALL OPINION.

GILLOTTS 170   SPEEDBALL FB3 FOR OUTLINE

VERY THICK LINE AROUND A PEN DRAWING.
THIS METHOD TRAPS THE PEN WORK, AND MAKES IT STAND OUT. WHAT'S HAPPENING HERE IS TURNING THE WHOLE THING INTO A DESIGN. THIS IS ABOUT AS THICK AS YOU SHOULD GO.

HERE IS AN EXAMPLE WHERE PUTTING PRESSURE ON A GILLOTTS 1290, A VERY *FLEXIBLE* PEN POINT, GIVES THE APPEARANCE OF BRUSH LINE. NEXT WAS ADDED A VERY FINE LINE, WHICH CONTRADICTS THE RULE OF **NOT** ADDING A FINE LINE AROUND A PEN DRAWING *!*

YOU CAN DECIDE FOR YOURSELF VERY SIMPLY... DO A DRAWING ON TRACING PAPER, USE A LIGHTBOX AND RETRACE IT FOUR OR FIVE TIMES ON BRISTOL, AND THEN INK EACH ONE A DIFFERENT WAY, UNTIL YOU COME UP WITH WHATEVER FEELS LIKE *FUN!*

MORE BRUSH

NO.2 BRUSH

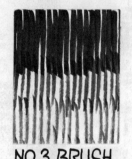

NO.3 BRUSH

NO.2 BRUSH

NO.2 BRUSH

NO.1 BRUSH

NO.2 BRUSH

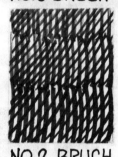

NO.2 BRUSH

NO.3 BRUSH

NO.3 BRUSH

NO.3 BRUSH

THIS CARTOON WAS DRAWN WITH A NO.1 BRUSH, AND A GILLOTTS 170 PEN

AND THE LETTERING WITH A B6 SPEEDBALL!

THE EXPERIMENT!

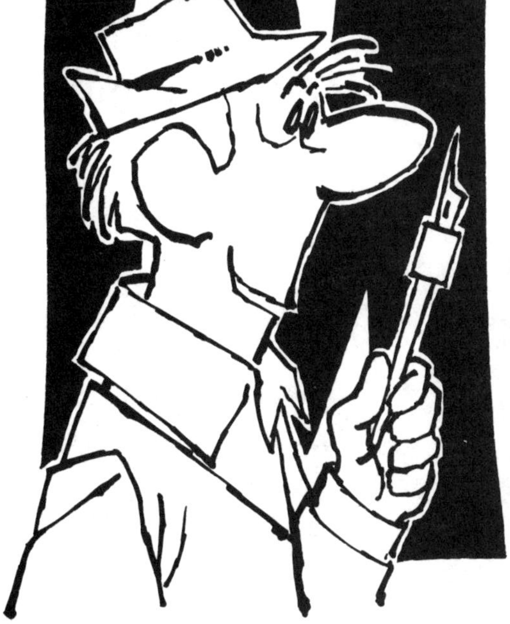

HERE'S HOW THE EXPERIMENT WAS DONE...

PROFESSIONAL CARTOONISTS WERE SENT THIS PENCIL DRAWING, DRAWN BY ME ...... AND WERE TOLD TO INK IT ANYWAY THEY SAW FIT, AND THEN FILL OUT A QUESTIONNAIRE AS TO THE TOOLS THEY USED, AND WHAT THEY ARE PRESENTLY DOING. THE RESULTS WERE FANTASTIC.

BELOW EACH INKED CARTOON IS THE INFORMATION ON THE PEN POINT, BRUSH, INK, AND ERASER USED BY THE CARTOONIST.

ALSO, FOR THE BENEFIT OF THE BEGINNING CARTOONIST, A 50% REDUCTION IS INSERTED BELOW THE ORIGINAL SIZE. SINCE MOST OF THE CARTOONISTS WORK AT LEAST TWICE UP, THEY CAN STUDY THE INKING AND SEE HOW THE LINES *HOLD* IN REDUCTION.

THE CARTOON IS PRINTED IN THE ORIGINAL SIZE AS INKED BY THE ARTIST SO THE STUDENT CAN STUDY PROFESSIONAL WORK.!

ORIGINAL SIZE

KEN MUSE

I LOVE DESIGN IN CARTOON-ING AND I LOVE TO INK! INKING IS THE CRAFT THAT GIVES A CARTOON THE POLISHED LOOK. *INKING IS LIKE GETTING DRESSED UP IN YOUR BEST CLOTHES. IF A ZIP PATTERN WILL MAKE MY CARTOON LOOK BETTER...I'LL USE IT! I ALWAYS EXPERIMENT.*

PEN POINT. *1290*

BRUSH . . . . . *ALL SIZES*

INK . . *HIGGINS E. DENSE*

ERASER . . . . *KNEADED*

I USED FORMATT NO. 7181 - 22 LINE, THEN I USED PRO-WHITE AND WORKED INTO A GRADATION!

50% REDUCTION

DAVE THORNE

HERE'S A GUY WITH GREAT CARTOONING STYLE, AND ESPECIALLY WITH ANIMALS. DAVE'S INKING IS REALLY SOMETHING TO BE ADMIRED. ANYTHING THAT WILL HOLD INK AND FLOWS ONTO THE PAPER WILL WORK FOR HIM. ADD THIS TO THE FACT HE LIVES IN HAWAII, AND IS A MEMBER OF THE HOUSE OF CARTOONS IN HONOLULU! *ALOHA!*

ORIGINAL SIZE

PEN POINT . . . . *NONE*
BRUSH . . *JAPANESE FUDE BRUSH PEN*
INK . . . . *SUMI*
ERASER . . . . . . *MAGIC RUB*

50% REDUCTION

ARMENTO

DONNA MARIE ARMENTO

DONNA IS A PROMISING YOUNG CARTOONIST THAT JUST WON'T GIVE UP. SHE FINISHED A HUGE MURAL IN A SHOPPING CENTER, LOADED WITH CARTOONS THAT WERE A JOY TO LOOK AT. SHE DOES SOME LOCAL FREELANCE AND HOPES SOMEDAY TO HAVE HER WORK SYNDICATED. CHECK-OUT HER CARTOONS FURTHER ON IN THIS CHAPTER.

ORIGINAL SIZE

PEN POINT... *A5 & 170*
BRUSH........ *NONE*
INK... *BLACK MAGIC*
ERASER.. *RUBKLEEN*

GOOD NEWS - DONNA IS NOW SYNDICATED WITH DICKSON-BENNETT. HER FEATURE IS "FINISH THE WORDS" PANEL

ARMENTO

50% REDUCTION

DON ARR CHRISTENSEN

DON IS A HAPPY-GO-LUCKY, FUNNY CARTOONIST. HE LOVES TO DRAW! HE SUBMITTED A BUNCH OF INK DRAWINGS... *ALL DIFFERENT.* I'VE DECIDED TO PRINT THREE. HE HAS A GREAT CARTOONING BOOK ON TIPS FROM TOP CARTOONISTS. CONTACT: *DONNAR PUBLICATIONS, 21790 YBARRA RD., WOODLAND HILLS, CALIF., 91364.....* YOU'LL NOTICE, DON HAS A GREAT STYLE FOR KID BOOKS... *WHICH HE DOES!*

Don Arr
(christensen)

ORIGINAL SIZE

PEN POINT. 659 CROQUIL AND FINE PENTEL STYLO BRUSH.. CHINESE FOX TAIL AND PENTEL 101 INK........ PELIKAN ERASER.... KNEADED

Don Arr
(christensen)

50% REDUCTION

52

Don Arr
(christensen)

Don Arr
(christensen)

ORIGINAL
SIZE

ORIGINAL
SIZE

50%
REDUCTION

50%
REDUCTION

LLOYD GOLA

ORIGINAL SIZE

LLOYD DID SOME STUFF FOR MAD MAGAZINE. YOU'LL NEVER FORGET HIS WORK ONCE YOU SEE IT. IT'S VERY DISTINCT AND ORIGINAL. LLOYD IS ONE OF THOSE GUYS WHO EATS AND SLEEPS DRAWING CARTOONS, AND HE'S A LOT OF FUN TO BE AROUND. NOTICE HIS DOUBLE LINES?
WE WENT TO ART SCHOOL TOGETHER IN DETROIT... AHH.. THOSE WERE THE DAYS.
YOU'LL FIND MORE OF LLOYD'S CARTOONS IN THIS CHAPTER.

PEN POINT.. 659 CROQUIL
BRUSH............. NONE
INK .... HIGGINS
ERASER..... KNEADED

LLOYD IS CREATIVE DIRECTOR FOR A MARKET COMMUNICATIONS GROUP, CREATIVE UNIVERSAL, IN SOUTHFIELD, MICHIGAN.

50% REDUCTION

54

CLIFF WIRTH

WE WENT TO ARTSCHOOL TOGETHER IN DETROIT. CLIFF IS AN EXCELLENT ALL-AROUND ARTIST-CARTOONIST, HE HAS DONE COLORING BOOKS, COMIC BOOKS, STRIPS, PANELS... *YOU NAME IT.* HE NEVER USES THE SAME PEN POINT MORE THAN ONCE.

ORIGINAL SIZE

PEN POINT.. *ALL OF THEM*

BRUSH... *ALL OF THEM*

INK ....*PELIKAN*

ERASER... *KNEADED*

CLIFF IS STAFF ARTIST FOR THE CHICAGO SUN TIMES.!

50% REDUCTION

JAMES MALONE

ORIGINAL SIZE

JAMES HAS A NICE ROMANCE GOING FOR INKING... I THINK HE LOVES IT AS MUCH AS DRAWING. THERE IS ALSO A CLEVER USE OF ZIP, ON THE PANTS. HE WORKS VERY HARD, OFTEN SPENDING LATE HOURS AT HIS BOARD.

PEN POINT.. *HUNT GLOBE*
BRUSH . . . . *NONE*
INK . . . . *HIGGINS*
ERASER . . . . *KNEADED*

JAMES WORKS AS A LAYOUT ARTIST FOR KMART INTERNATIONAL HEAD-QUARTERS, TROY, MICHIGAN. HE ALSO DOES "RALPH'S POST" COMIC STRIP!

50% REDUCTION

ORIGINAL SIZE

BOB TAYLOR

BOB HAS DONE A LOT OF WORK FOR COMIC BOOKS, AND HAS DEVELOPED INTO A GREAT CARTOONIST, AND WORKS JUST AS WELL WITH A BRUSH AS HE DOES WITH A PEN! THIS BEAUTIFUL INKING JOB WAS DONE WITH A BRUSH.... AND NOTICE HOW WELL HIS INK LINES TAKE REDUCTION.

BOB LIVES IN MICHIGAN. HIS HOBBIES ARE ART COLLECTION, BACKPACKING, WATER SPORTS, PART-TIME CRIME FIGHTER!

PEN POINT.... *CROQUIL*
BRUSH.... *NOS. 2 AND 5*
INK.. *FW WATERPROOF*
ERASER.... *KNEADED*

BOB DRAWS TWO STRIPS FOR NATIONAL LAMPOON: *"TIMBERLAND TALES"*, AND *"THE APPLETONS."*

50% REDUCTION

LARRY WRIGHT

. . . . HAS A GREAT POLISHED STYLE OF CARTOONING THAT TAKES *REDUC-TIONS BEAUTIFULLY.* THE CHANGES HE MADE IN THE ORIGINAL CARTOON ARE FUNNY, AND SHOW GREAT STYLE AND ORIGINALITY. LARRY HAS TWO NATIONALLY SYNDICATED FEATURES: "KIT 'N CARLYLE", WITH NEA, AND "WRIGHT ANGLES", WITH UNITED FEATURES. HE ALSO DOES 3 EDITORIAL CARTOONS A WEEK FOR THE DETROIT NEWS.. *AND I THOUGHT I WAS BUSY!*

ORIGINAL SIZE

PEN POINT... *HUNT #56*
BRUSH .... *NONE*
INK .... *PELIKAN*
ERASER .. *PINK PEARL*

MORE OF LARRY'S CARTOONING APPEARS IN THIS CHAPTER *!*

50% REDUCTION

GEORGE CRIONAS

GEORGE AND I WENT THROUGH SCHOOL TOGETHER IN DETROIT. AFTER HIGHSCHOOL, GEORGE LEFT FOR CALIFORNIA AND BECAME A PROFESSIONAL ACTOR. BESIDES ACTING, GEORGE DID A LOT OF FREE-LANCE AND BECAME AN OUTSTANDING AND WELL-KNOWN CLOWN ARTIST, IN PEN AND INK, OILS, AND ACRYLIC, AND HAS HAD MANY ONE-MAN SHOWS, CURRENTLY, ONE IN NEW YORK. MORE OF GEORGE'S WORK IN THIS CHAPTER OF THE BOOK!

ORIGINAL SIZE

50% REDUCTION

PEN POINT..... CROQUIL
BRUSH.... NO.3 SABLE
INK.......... ARTONE
ERASER..... ARTGUM

CONTACT GEORGE AT 4753 ABARGO ST.
WOODLAND HILLS, CALIFORNIA • 91364

LEO STOUTSENBERGER

LEO IS ONE OF THE MOST COMPETENT CARTOONISTS I'VE EVER KNOWN, AND ALSO A PROFESSIONAL WATERCOLORIST. HE IS DIRECTOR OF "CARTOONERAMA", (A CARTOONIST CORRESPONDENCE COURSE), AND ASSOCIATE PROFESSOR OF FINE ARTS AT PAIER COLLEGE OF ART IN CONNECTICUT. HE HAS AUTHORED "CONTROLLED WATERCOLOR", AND IS NOW WORKING ON HIS SECOND BOOK ON WATERCOLOR. LEO IS A MEMBER OF THE NATIONAL CARTOONISTS SOCIETY, AND CONN. WATERCOLOR SOCIETY.

ORIGINAL SIZE

50% REDUCTION

PEN POINT..... *HUNT 22*
BRUSH.. *#2 W.+N. SABLE*
INK............. *HIGGINS*
ERASER....... *KNEADED*

REACH LEO AT 41 ORCHARD HILL ROAD, BRANFORD, CT. 06405

ROY PAUL NELSON

ROY HAS AN INTERESTING STYLE OF DRAWING. (HE IS IN MY "SECRETS OF PROFESSIONAL CARTOONING" BOOK), AND I WAS CURIOUS TO SEE HOW HE WOULD INK MY STYLE OF CARTOONING. HE HAS EIGHT BOOKS TO HIS CREDIT. THREE ON CARTOONING!
ROY IS A PROFESSOR OF JOURNALISM AT THE UNIVERSITY OF OREGON, AND A GRAPHIC DESIGN CONSULTANT....
OF COURSE HE'S WORKING ON A NEW BOOK!

ORIGINAL SIZE

PEN POINT... MONT BLANC
CLASSIC FOUNTAIN PEN
BRUSH.. #1 WINSOR-NEWTON
INK.. MONT BLANC/PELICAN
ERASER.... PINK PEARL

50% REDUCTION

ORIGINAL SIZE

SHARON SHIMAZU

SHARON IS AN UP AND COMING TALENT WITH ORIGINAL IDEAS AND GREAT CARTOONING. SHE DOES CARTOONS FOR THE EAST-WEST JOURNAL MAGAZINE, AND EDITORIAL CARTOONS FOR THE EAST-WEST NEWSPAPER IN HAWAII. KEEPING ACTIVE IN HER PROFESSION TAKES LONG HOURS AT THE BOARD, BUT SHARON MANAGES TO KEEP BUSY IN VARIOUS FREELANCE PROJECTS! MORE OF SHARON'S CARTOONING APPEARS IN THIS CHAPTER.

PEN POINT... *S. BALL 5½ AND 0.3 RAPIDOGRAPH*
BRUSH........*NONE*
INK. *HIGGINS B. MAGIC*
ERASER.. *KNEADED*

50% REDUCTION

BILL HOEST

BILL IS ANOTHER CARTOONIST WITH A VERY DISTINCT STYLE, AND WHEN HE INKS, AS YOU CAN SEE, HE DOESN'T FOOL AROUND. BILL DRAWS THE "LOCKHORNS" FOR KING FEATURES, AND FREELANCES THE GAG PANEL MARKET EXTENSIVELY. I SEE HIS WORK EVERYWHERE... AND IT'S ALWAYS FUNNY. BILL ALSO DOES ART FOR ENCYCLOPEDIAS AND TEXTBOOKS. YOU CAN IMAGINE THE HOURS HE SPENDS AT THE BOARD!

ORIGINAL SIZE

PEN POINT... *CROQUIL AND SPEEDBALL*
BRUSH.... *#2 THRU #6*
INK........... *INDIA*
ERASER... *KNEADED*

50% REDUCTION

63

ORIGINAL SIZE

BILL MEADOR

BILL AND I WENT TO THE SAME ART SCHOOL IN DETROIT, BUT AT DIFFERENT TIMES. BILL IS AN ILLUSTRATOR AND CAN DRAW UP A STORM. HE IS ALSO A CAPABLE AUTOMOTIVE DESIGNER AND TECHNICAL ILLUSTRATOR, AND INTO COMPUTER GRAPHICS. I ASKED BILL (WHO TEACHES COMMERCIAL ART WITH ME), TO INK THE CARTOON FOR A COMPARISON WITH A PRO-FESSIONAL CARTOONIST.....
AN INTERESTING STYLE!

PEN POINT.. *GILLOTTS 170*
BRUSH.. *W&N #3 SERIES 7*
INK... *HIGGINS NO. 4465*
ERASER.... *KNEADED*

BESIDES TEACHING COMMERCIAL ART AND PHOTOGRAPHY AT MACOMB COMMUNITY COLLEGE IN MICHIGAN, BILL DOES MUCH FREELANCE WORK!

50% REDUCTION

ORIGINAL SIZE

MATT CHAMPLIN

MATT IS AN ENGINEER FOR THE FORD MOTOR CO. IN DEARBORN, MICHIGAN. HE DOES A LOT OF FREE-LANCING FOR LOCAL AGENCIES DOING CARTOONS AND LOGO DESIGNS. MATT HAS A CLEAN STYLE, FINE PEN WORK, AND GOOD PLACEMENT OF BLACKS. HE'S JUST RECENTLY ENTERED THE GAG PANEL FIELD. BESIDES ALL THIS, HE TEACHES ADULT EDUCATION CARTOONING CLASSES AND CHALK-TALKS FOR ADULT AND CHILDREN SHOWS.

PEN POINT *GILLOTTS 1950*
BRUSH .. *W&N #1 SERIES 7*
INK . . . . *HIGGINS*
ERASER . . . . *KNEADED*

IDEA METHOD: HE PICKS UP ON WHAT OTHERS SAY, AND USES WORD ASSO-CIATION (PEOPLE, PLACES, THINGS) AND STANDARD COMIC SITUATIONS!

50% REDUCTION

PAUL GRINGLE

PAUL HAS BEEN IN CARTOONING ALL OF HIS LIFE, AND IS WHAT WE CALL A "CARTOONIST'S CARTOONIST." HE HAS DONE ALL KINDS OF THINGS, INCLUDING COMIC STRIPS, ANIMATION, PANELS, GREETING CARDS, COMIC BOOKS, TABLE CLOTHS, NAPKINS, T-SHIRTS, MATCHBOOKS, ETC, ETC, ETC.

ORIGINAL SIZE

PEN POINT 1290
BRUSH NO.3
INK . . . . PELIKAN
ERASER . . . . KNEADED

PAUL IS COMICS EDITOR FOR DICKSON-BENNETT INTERNATIONAL FEATURES INTERNATIONAL SYND.

PAUL HAS BEEN SYNDICATED IN OVER 650 NEWSPAPERS. HE DID "OUT OUR WAY," "THE WILLETS," "RURAL DELIVERLY," "HOW WYN SOCK SAVED CHRISTMAS"

50% REDUCTION

SEVENTEEN
CARTOONISTS

DRAW
UP
A
STORM!

GEORGE CRIONAS

GEORGE CRIONAS
© 1982

PERMISSION FROM GEORGE CRIONAS

GEORGE WORKS WITH AN INSTAMATIC CAMERA AND SKETCHPAD WHEN HE GOES TO "CLOWN ALLEY" OF RINGLING BROS. CIRCUS TO GATHER HIS MATERIAL FOR HIS CLOWN SUBJECTS...THEN BACK TO HIS STUDIO FOR WORK IN OIL, ACRYLIC, AND ETCHINGS. HE TALKS TO CLOWNS, GATHERING GAGS, STUNTS, AND COMEDY ROUTINES. GEORGE SAYS IF YOU HAVE GOD-GIVEN TALENTS, NEVER BE DISCOURAGED. REJECTION IS PART OF LIFE. JUST WHEN YOU THINK ALL IS HOPELESS...THE DOOR OPENS!

AGE YOU STARTED TO DRAW: 5

HOW LONG PUBLISHED: 15 YRS.

COLLEGE: NONE

ART SCHOOL: JEPSON & PRIVATELY

FAR AHEAD YOU WORK: 6 MOS.

HOW MANY AT ONE TIME: 3

DO YOU DRAW LINES AROUND ART: YES   ZIP: NO

FINAL ART DRAWN ON: FABRIANO ARTISTICO   WASH: YES

LIGHTBOX: YES   PENCIL GRADE: NO.2   INK: ARTONE

ERASER: ARTGUM   PEN POINTS FOR INKING: CROQUIL

PENPOINT FOR LETTERING: A5   BRUSH: NO.3 SABLE

TIME FOR DRAWING ONE PANEL: 2 HRS.   FREELANCE: YES

BESIDES HIS ACTING AND DRAWING, GEORGE'S HOBBY IS PLAYING THE GUITAR. A VERY LARGE PERCENTAGE OF ARTISTS ARE MUSICIANS!

EVEN IN A 35% REDUCTION, GEORGE'S INK LINES *HOLD!* MANY BEGINNING CARTOONISTS NEVER SEEM TO UNDERSTAND HOW IMPORTANT THIS IS. THE NEXT PAGE IS A SECTION OF THE 18 X 24, *PRINTED ORIGINAL SIZE.*

GEORGE'S WORK HAS APPEARED IN THE FOLLOWING :

1972 COVER OF NATIONAL THEATER MAGAZINE • SUNDAY DETROIT NEWS SUPPLEMENT-1975 • PATRICIAN PUBLICATIONS-CHICAGO • COLLIER ART CORP-LOS ANGELES • FIDELITY ARTS-LOS ANGELES • MARTIN LAWRENCE GALLERIES & BEVERLY HILLS GALLERY-LA.

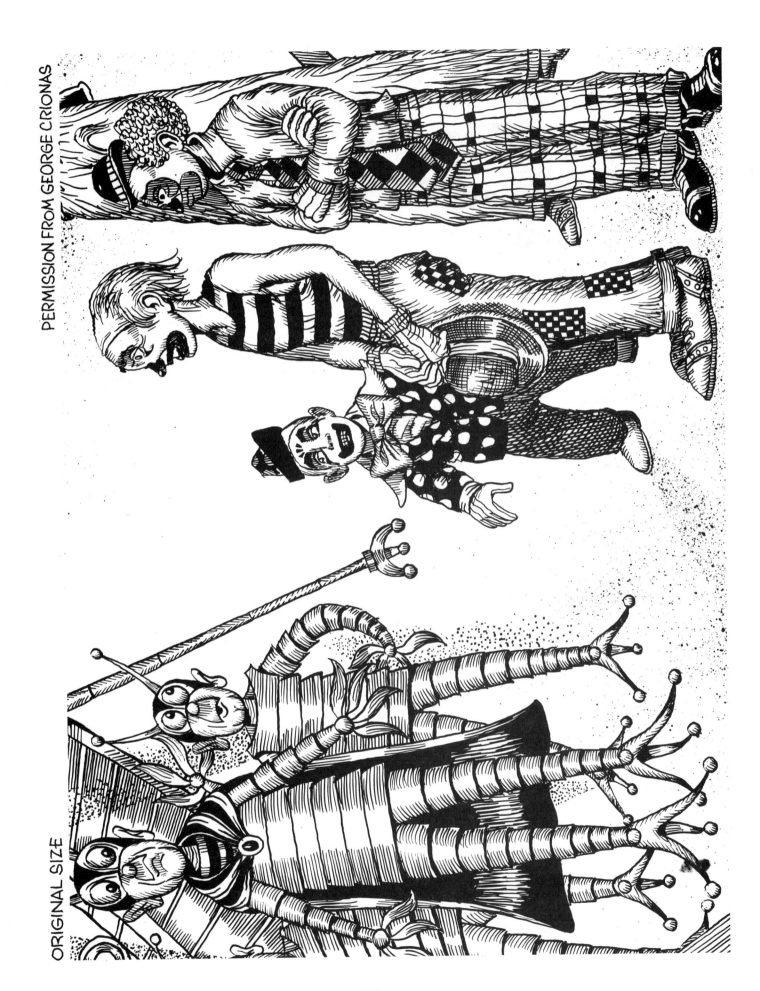

ORIGINAL SIZE

71

BILL SEELBACH

Uh.... Whell.... IN ORDER TO BALANCE THE BUDGET WE INTEND TO DECREASE FEDERAL SPENDING BY PUMPING BILLIONS OF EXTRA DOLLARS INTO DEFENSE SO AS TO ACHIEVE NUCLEAR ARMS REDUCTION.... THEN BY CREATING FEWER JOBS WE INTEND TO LOWER THE UNEMPLOYMENT RATE.... THEN....

PERMISSION FROM BILL SEELBACH

I'M INCLUDING BILL AS A PROMISING YOUNG CARTOONING STUDENT FROM MY CLASS IN ART SCHOOL. HE HAS A LOT OF TALENT AND GREAT IDEAS. BILL HOPES, LIKE ALL CARTOONISTS, ONE DAY TO BE A SYNDICATED EDITORIAL CARTOONIST!

BILL READS AS MUCH AS HE CAN — NEWSPAPERS, JOURNALS, MAGAZINES, AND OTHER EDITORIAL CARTOONISTS, PLUS NEWS ON RADIO AND TV!

AGE YOU STARTED TO DRAW: *AS SOON AS I COULD HOLD PENCIL*

HOW LONG PUBLISHED: *1 YR.*   COLLEGE: *MACOMB COLLEGE, MICH.*

ART SCHOOL: *MACOMB COLLEGE*   FAR AHEAD YOU WORK: *2-3 DAYS*

HOW MANY AT ONE TIME: *1*   LINES AROUND ART: *SOMETIMES*

FINAL ART DRAWN ON: *OHIO GRAPHICS DUO-SHADE* ZIP: *NOPE*

WASH: *NOPE* LIGHTBOX: *YES*   PENCIL GRADE: *H PENCILS*

INK: *KOH-I-NOOR* ERASER: *RED RUBY AND KNEADED*

PEN POINT FOR INKING: *KOH-I-NOOR ART PEN AND #290*

PEN POINT FOR LETTERING: *KOH-I-NOOR ART PEN*

ORIGINAL SIZE

BILL SKETCHES OUT ROUGHS ON SCRAP PAPER FOR HIS BASIC LAYOUT, THEN CLEANS IT UP ON TRACING PAPER. HE THEN USES A LIGHTBOX FOR FINAL ART, INKING DIRECTLY ON THE BOARD. HIS ADVICE FOR ASPIRING CARTOONISTS IS TO **GO FOR IT!** PUSH A PEN AND LET IT HAPPEN. BILL'S EDITORIAL CARTOONS APPEAR IN "THE SOURCE" NEWSPAPER IN UTICA, MICHIGAN.

BILL'S HOBBY IS PLAYING GUITAR, AND WRITING COMEDY!

TOMMY TRUEHEART

© DONNA ARMENTO

DONNA ARMENTO

METHOD OF WORKING: **I LOCK MYSELF IN THE DEN, AND PRETEND I'M A FAMOUS CARTOONIST WITH A SYNDICATE.**

METHOD FOR GETTING IDEAS: I DON'T HAVE A SPECIAL METHOD.... THEY JUST COME TO ME. HOWEVER, I'VE BEEN HIT OVER THE HEAD MANY TIMES BY MY SISTER, WHEN SHE GETS MAD AT ME!

ADVICE: **THAT'S EASY... JUST NEVER GIVE UP!**

© DONNA ARMENTO

ORIGINAL SIZE

AGE YOU STARTED TO DRAW: 5 COLLEGE: *NONE* ART SCHOOL: *NONE*

HOW MANY AT ONE TIME: *2 PER DAY* LINES AROUND ART: *YES*

FINAL ART ON: *GRUMBACHER PLATE FINISH* ZIP: *7001-7003*

WASH: *NONE* DO YOU USE LIGHTBOX: *YES* PENCIL: *NO. 3*

INK: *HIGGINS BLACK MAGIC* ERASER: *RUBKLEEN*

PEN POINTS FOR DRAWING: *A5 SPEEDBALL AND GILLOTTS 170*

PEN POINTS FOR LETTERING: *A5 AND B5* BRUSH: *A BIG ONE*

HOW LONG FOR ONE PANEL: *4-5 HOURS* SYNDICATE: *SOME DAY*

LIVE IN WHICH STATE: *MICHIGAN* FREELANCE: *YES*

HOBBY: *SLEEPING, EATING, AND CARTOONING!*

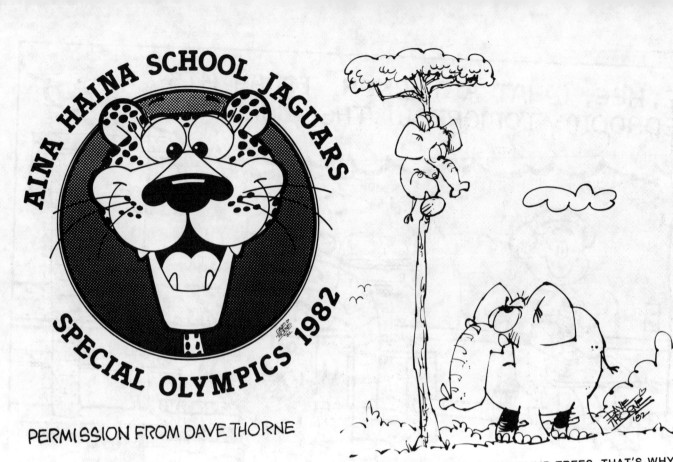

AINA HAINA SCHOOL JAGUARS

SPECIAL OLYMPICS 1982

PERMISSION FROM DAVE THORNE

BECAUSE ELEPHANTS CAN'T CLIMB TREES, THAT'S WHY!

DAVE THORNE

AGE STARTED TO DRAW: *VERY EARLY*   ART SCHOOL: *CHOUINARD ART INST.*

PUBLISHED: *1950'S* FAR AHEAD: *UP TO DEADLINE*   AT ONE TIME: *VARIES*

LINES AROUND ART: *SOMETIMES*   FINAL ON: *2 & 3 PLY BRISTOL-KID*

ZIP: *OCCASIONALLY* WASH: *RARELY*   LIGHTBOX: *SOMETIMES*

PENCIL: *2H, H, 2, B* INK: *SUMI (JAPANESE) AND HIGGINS INK*

ERASER: *MAGIC RUB* PEN FOR LETTERING: *B6, PENTEL SIGN PEN*

PEN POINTS FOR DRAWING: *RAPIDOGRAPH, B6, FELT PENS, FUDE PEN*

BRUSH: *5 & 7* HOW LONG FOR ONE PANEL: *COUPLE OF MIN. TO 1 HOUR*

STATE: *HAWAII* FREELANCE: *YES*   SYNDICATE: *NONE*

WHAT'S FOR LUNCH?

PERMISSION FROM DAVE THORNE

DAVE'S HOBBIES ARE CARTOONING, PIANO, FRIENDS, AND COLLECTING ORIGINAL ART!

ORIGINAL SIZE

DAVE'S METHOD OF WORKING: USUALLY ROUGH QUICKLY & LIGHTLY W/ PENCIL-VERY FREE & LOOSE, THEN GO OVER QUICKLY W/ JAPANESE FUDE BRUSH PEN FOR INKING FOR PRECISE WORK, I SPEND MORE TIME ON PENCIL ROUGH THEN INK MORE DELIBERATELY WITH PEN— USUALLY FELT TIPS & TECH PENS. I HAVE USED TEMPLATES & TECH PENS ON SLICK ONES! HOW DO I GET IDEAS? START DRAWING AND IDEAS COME. GET WITH OTHER CARTOONISTS AND BOUNCE OFF IDEAS. SOMETIMES METHODS FROM KEN MUSE'S "SECRETS OF PROFESSIONAL CARTOONING". SOMETIMES DURING MEDITATION OR RUNNING.. SOMETIMES OTHER CARTOON-ISTS' WORK INSPIRES ME!

WHAT'S FOR LUNCH?

50% REDUCTION

ADVICE: DRAW! DRAW! DRAW! STUDY WORK OF OTHERS, MEET OTHER CARTOONISTS, STUDY HUMOR, LISTEN TO HUMORISTS, ANALYZE, STUDY ANATOMY AND DRAW, DRAW, DRAW, DRAW, DRAW, DRAW, DRAW, DRAW, DRAW, DRAW, DRAW, DRAW, DRAW!

BUT WHY CAN'T WE JUST WAKE HIM UP SO I CAN SIT ON THE COUCH, TOO?

3-12
© 1982 by NEA, Inc.

PERMISSION FROM NEA

LARRY WRIGHT

LARRY DIDN'T MENTION HIS METHOD FOR GETTING IDEAS, BUT HE SPENDS LOTS OF TIME LOOKING OUT WINDOWS.

AGE YOU STARTED TO DRAW: *TEN*   **COLLEGE:** *NONE*

ART SCHOOL: *NONE* **HOW LONG PUBLISHED:** *22 YEARS*

FAR AHEAD YOU WORK: *7 TO 14 WEEKS* **ZIP:** *RARELY*

HOW MANY AT ONE TIME: *VARIES*   **WASH:** *RARELY*

FINAL ART DRAWN ON: *2 PLY STRATHMORE* **INK:** *PELIKAN*

DO YOU USE A LIGHTBOX: *OCCASIONALLY* **BRUSH:** *NONE*

PENCIL GRADE: *HB*   **PEN POINTS FOR INKING:** *HUNT #56*

PEN POINTS FOR LETTERING: *DESIGN ART MARKER 229-LV*

HOW LONG TO DRAW ONE PANEL: *10 TO 15 MINUTES*

HOBBY: *MODEL TRAINS AND GOLF*

WHAT STATE DO YOU LIVE: *MICHIGAN*

ARE YOU FREELANCE: *NO*

ADVICE FOR ASPIRING CARTOONISTS: *SEE NEXT PAGE*

PERMISSION FROM NEA   ORIGINAL SIZE

LARRY'S ADVICE FOR ASPIRING CARTOONISTS:

"GIVE IT UP. THERE ARE FAR TOO MANY CARTOONISTS AS IT IS. GET INTO VIDEO GAMES AND T-SHIRTS, THAT'S WHERE THE FUTURE LIES."

SHARON SHIMAZU

SHARON'S STRIP APPEARS IN THE HAWAII HERALD. SHE IS A TALENTED *UP-AND-COMING CARTOONIST!* HER METHOD OF WORKING IS DRAWING LIGHTLY, FIRST IN PENCIL, DIRECTLY ON THE BRISTOL...THEN INKING! ABOUT HALF THE PROFESSIONALS WORK THIS WAY... *THE OTHER HALF WORK WITH LIGHTBOXES.*

AGE YOU STARTED TO DRAW: *4*   HOW LONG PUBLISHED: *1 YEAR*

COLLEGE: *INT. CHRISTIAN., UNIV. of TOKYO*   ART SCHOOL: *UNIV of ARIZ.*

FAR AHEAD YOU WORK: *NOT VERY*   HOW MANY AT ONCE: *NOT VERY*

ZIP: *RARELY*   FINAL ART ON: *2 PLY BAINBRIDGE or STRATHMORE*

WASH: *SOMETIMES*   LIGHTBOX: *SOMETIMES*   PENCIL GRADE: *3B*

INK: *HIGGINS BLACK MAGIC*   ERASER: *KNEADED*   BRUSH: *NO.1*

PEN POINTS FOR INKING: *HUNT 107-B5½*   FREELANCE: *YES*

PEN POINTS FOR LETTERING: *0.3 RAPIDOGRAPH*

TIME TO DRAW ONE STRIP: *1-2 HRS.*   LINES AROUND ART: *YES*

ORIGINAL SIZE

PERMISSION FROM SHARON SHIMAZU

SHARON'S METHOD OF WORKING:

"I DAYDREAM CONSTANTLY."

HER ADVICE FOR ASPIRING CARTOONISTS:

"BELIEVE IN YOURSELF- *A LOT*- AND ACT ON THAT BELIEF."

SHARON'S WORK HAS APPEARED IN THE FOLLOWING:

THE HAWAII HERALD · EAST-WEST JOURNAL JAPANESE NEWSPAPER · EAST-WEST PHOTO JOURNAL MAGAZINE · THE HONOLULU STAR-BULLETIN · HAWAII STATE-TEACHERS ASSOCIATION NEWSPAPER... *SHARON'S HOBBY IS OIL PAINTING!*

Don Arr

DON DOES A ROUGH FOR LIGHTBOX TRANSFER TO FINISH PAPER (IF NOT USING ILL. BOARD), AND THEN INKS THE DRAWING USING PEN OR BRUSH. THEN HE ERASES THE PENCIL! DON SAYS YOU GOTTA KEEP GRASPING AT EVERY OPPORTUNITY.

AGE YOU STARTED TO DRAW: *FIVE*   HOW LONG PUBLISHED: *39 YRS.*

COLLEGE: *NONE*   FAR AHEAD YOU WORK: *WHATEVER FITS JOB*

ART SCHOOL: *MINNEAPOLIS SCH. of ART & FEDERAL SCHOOL*

HOW MANY AT ONE TIME: *ONE*   LINES AROUND ART: *SOMETIMES*

FINAL ART ON: *STRATHMORE 2 PLY PLATE*   ZIP: *RARELY*

WASH: *OCCASIONALLY*   LIGHTBOX: *SOME*   PENCIL GRADE: *2B*

INK: *PELIKAN*   ERASER: *KNEADED*   BRUSH: *PENTEL 101 FOXTAIL*

PEN POINTS FOR DRAWING: *ASSORTED*   LETTERING: *STILL LOOKING*

IN WHAT STATE DO YOU LIVE: *CALIFORNIA*   FREELANCE: *YES*

HOBBY: *OIL PAINTING*   ARE YOU SYNDICATED: *NO*

METHODS FOR GETTING IDEAS

JUST SIT AND MULL.... (THE PARTICULAR AREA OR PROBLEM) "HMM...MAYBE BUGS BUNNY GETS HIT BY A BUTTERNUT THAT MUST BE FROM THE BUTTER PLANET."

IT'S NOT EASY BEING A **DUCK**!

PERMISSION FROM DON R. CHRISTENSEN

ORIGINAL SIZE

Don Arr

I JEST MISSED BEIN' THE ONE THAT WON THE WEST!

ANYBODY CAN BE A **CARTOONIST**, IS WHAT THE MAN SAYS!

ORIGINAL SIZE

Don Arr

Don Arr

STACY By Randy Bisson

© DICKSON-BENNETT 1982

Bisson

"I DON'T REMEMBER SEEING YOUR NAME ON THE GUEST LIST!"

RANDY BISSON

RANDY JUST SITS DOWN AND DRAWS CARTOONS! HIS STYLE IS SIMPLE AND RIGHT TO THE POINT. HE DRAWS ONLY WHAT IS NEEDED, AND LEAVES THE REST OUT!

RANDY DOES A ROUGH ON TYPING PAPER, THEN HE TRACES DIRECTLY WITH A RAPIDOGRAPH #2 ONTO HEAVY MOUNTI MATTE VIA LIGHTBOX...THEN ADDS CAPTION.

AGE YOU STARTED TO DRAW: *FIVE*   HOW LONG PUBLISHED: *12 YRS.*

COLLEGE: *NONE*   ART SCHOOL: *NONE*   USE A LIGHTBOX: *YES*

HOW MANY AT ONE TIME: *12*   ZIP: *SOMETIMES, FORMATT 7000*

WASH: *NO*   PENCIL GRADE: *NO. 2*   INK: *KOH-I-NOOR*   BRUSH: *5*

ERASER: *EBERHARD FABER*   HOW LONG FOR ONE PANEL: *1-5 HRS.*

PEN POINTS FOR DRAWING: *RAPIDOGRAPH #2*   LETTERING: *#3*

WHERE DO YOU LIVE: *SPOKANE, WASH.*   FREELANCE: *MAGAZINES*

HOBBY: *COLLECTING ORIGINAL COMIC ART*

RANDY'S METHOD FOR GETTING IDEAS IS WATCHING HIS LITTLE GIRL. HE ALSO READS EVERY CARTOON AND COMIC HE CAN GET HIS HANDS ON... HE'S USUALLY ABLE TO SWITCH AND TWIST GAGS TO FIT HIS "STACY" PANEL.

HIS ADVICE FOR ASPIRING CARTOONISTS IS *PRACTICE CONSTANTLY AND NEVER GIVE UP.* MAKE SURE YOUR WORK LOOKS PROFESSIONAL AND COMPARES TO THE ONES YOU SEE IN THE MAJOR MAGAZINES AND COMIC PAGES — THAT'S YOUR DIRECT COMPETITION!

© DICKSON-BENNETT 1982

PERMISSION FROM DICKSON-BENNETT

ORIGINAL SIZE

Bisson

JACK BARRETT

JACK IS CERTAINLY A MASTER OF HIS PROFESSION. HIS FINE ART WORK IS TO BE ADMIRED BY THOSE WHO ENTER THE PROFESSION. HIS ADVICE: "TO BEGIN WITH—YOU MUST HAVE A FOUNDATION IN DRAWING. THIS TO ME IS ALL IMPORTANT. BE YOURSELF, AND OF COURSE HAVE SOMETHING TO SAY, THE MORE UNIQUE THE BETTER."

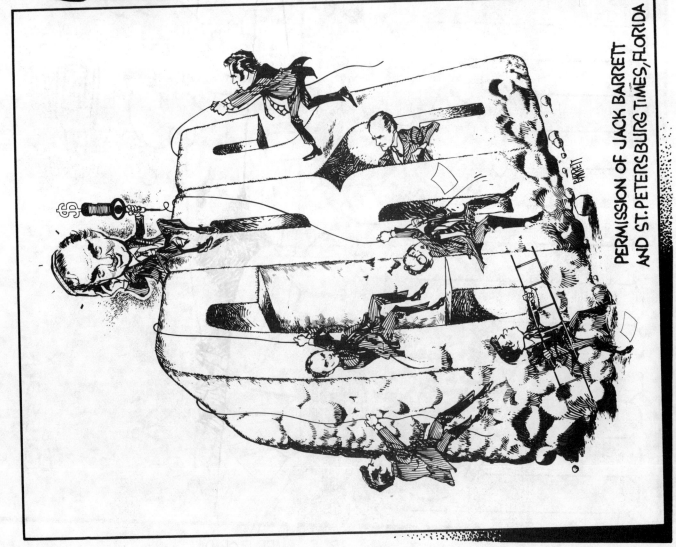

PERMISSION OF JACK BARRETT AND ST. PETERSBURG TIMES, FLORIDA

ORIGINAL SIZE

JACK'S WORK HAS APPEARED IN "KING AND MAYFAIR", MAGAZINES OF SATIRICAL WORKS IN THE UNITED KINGDOM. ALSO 2 BOOKS PUBLISHED-CARTOONS. "HANDS DOWN" AND "LAXATIVE". NEWSFEATURES, SPORTS, PORTRAITS, FOR ST. PETERSBURG TIMES, 12 YEARS!

MORE ABOUT JACK BARRETT

AGE YOU STARTED TO DRAW: 7 YRS.

ART SCHOOL: ART INSTITUTE OF PITTSBURGH

HOW LONG PUBLISHED: 12 YRS.   HOBBY: DRAWING-PAINTING

HOW FAR AHEAD DO YOU WORK: DAILY

HOW MANY DO YOU DRAW AT ONE TIME: ONE

DO YOU DRAW LINES AROUND ART: AT TIMES

FINAL ART DRAWN ON: STRATHMORE 4 PLY

WASH: IF JOB REQUIRES   LIGHTBOX: NO   ZIP: YES

PENCIL GRADE: 4H   INK: HIGGINS   ERASER: SOFT

PEN POINTS FOR DRAWING: CROQUIL   BRUSH: 2-4

PEN POINTS FOR LETTERING: SPEEDBALL

NEWSPAPER: ST. PETERSBURG TIMES, FLORIDA - 12 YRS.

HOW LONG TO DRAW ONE PANEL: 5 HOURS

METHOD OF WORKING:

I SELDOM MAKE ROUGHS, GOING DIRECTLY TO THE BOARD OR 4 PLY AND PENCIL— IF TIME ALLOWS I WILL DO A NUMBER OF SKETCHES. IF TIME IS SHORT I'LL COMPOSE IN MY MIND.

METHOD FOR GETTING IDEAS:

A STORY IS ALWAYS SUBMITTED BEFOREHAND. SUGGESTIONS MAY BE GIVEN BY THE EDITOR/OR WRITER! I MAY READ THE STORY MANY TIMES BEFORE PICTURES APPEAR. THIS PROCESS VARIES. SOMETIMES NO STORY!

PERMISSION FROM BOB TAYLOR

BOB TAY LOR

BOY CARTOONIST!

BOB DOES PAPERBACK BOOKS, MONTHLY ILLUSTRATIONS FOR SCHOLAS-
TIC PUBLISHING, DYNAMITE, HOT DOG, BANANAS MAGAZINE, TV
PILOTS FOR WALT DISNEY, ABC, AND CABLE TELEVISION.

AGE YOU STARTED TO DRAW: *TWO*   COLLEGE: *NONE*

ART SCHOOL: *CENTER FOR CREATIVE STUDIES, DETROIT*

HOW LONG PUBLISHED: *15 YEARS* FAR AHEAD YOU WORK: *3 MOS.*

AT ONE TIME: *ONE* LINES AROUND ART: *YES* ZIP: *DEPENDS*

FINAL ART DRAWN ON: *ART-TEC BOARD, MEDIUM SURFACE*

WASH: *WHEN THE ART DEMANDS*   A LIGHTBOX: *RARELY*

PEN GRADE: *MECHANICAL PENCIL 0.5mm 2H LEAD*

INK: *FW WATERPROOF* ERASER: *KNEADED MAGIC RUB*

PEN POINTS FOR DRAWING: *CROQUIL* LETTERING: *A5*

BRUSH: *#2 STRATHMORE KOLINSKY FOR INK, #5 FOR WASH*

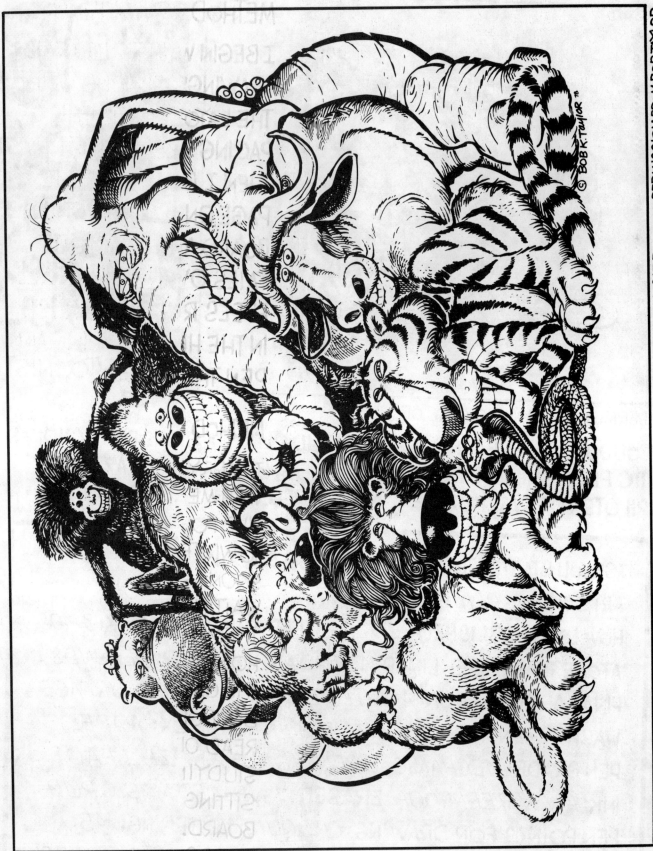

METHOD OF WORKING:

I BEGIN WITH THUMB NAIL DRAWINGS, PLAYING WITH THE LAYOUT UNTIL THE PACING FEELS RIGHT. THEN I BLUE LINE THE PAGE ON ILLUSTRATION BOARD AND PENCIL DETAILS OVER THIS. IF ALL FEELS RIGHT, I BRUSH IN THE HEAVIER LINE AND PEN THE DETAIL.

METHOD FOR GETTING IDEAS:

I CARRY A SKETCH BOOK WITH ME TO JOT DOWN IDEAS. I'VE FOUND IT IMPORTANT TO WRITE IDEAS DOWN AS SOON AS POSSIBLE .... WAITING OR COMMITTING THEM TO MEMORY SOMEHOW LOSES THE PUNCH OF THE GAG. IF I'VE HAD AN UNPRODUCTIVE WEEK, I READ OR WANDER ABOUT STUDYING PEOPLE BEFORE SITTING DOWN AT THE BOARD. I WORK BACKWARDS FROM PUNCHLINE TO INTRO.

PERMISSION FROM LLOYD GOLA

LLOYD GOLA

LLOYD HAS BEEN IN SLIDE FILMS EVER SINCE HE LEFT ART SCHOOL! DOING FILMS FOR GENERAL MOTORS, FORD, AND CHRYSLER. *A LOT OF WORK!*

METHOD FOR GETTING IDEAS: USUALLY CLIENTS SUPPLY THE SCRIPT—FOR MAD, IT WAS JUST STARING OUT THE WINDOW AND THINKING: "WHAT IS FUNNY—WHAT WOULD THEY BUY?" THE FIRST THOUGHTS ARE USUALLY BEST!

AGE YOU STARTED TO DRAW: *FIVE*   ART SCHOOL: *MEINZINGER, DETROIT*
COLLEGE: *NONE* FINAL ART DRAWN ON: *STRATHMORE, 2 AND 3 PLY*
ZIPATONE: *SELDOM* WASH: *NO* DO YOU USE A LIGHTBOX: *YES*
PENCILS: *H AND F*   INK: *HIGGINS*   ERASER: *KNEADED*
PEN POINTS FOR DRAWING FINAL ART: *GILLOTTS 659 CROQUIL*
PEN POINTS FOR LETTERING: *SPEEDBALL B6 AND B5½*
BRUSH: *NO. 2*   IN WHICH STATE DO YOU LIVE: *MICHIGAN*

PERMISSION FROM LLOYD GOLA

ADVICE FOR ASPIRING CARTOONISTS: *WORK!* GET MAD MAGAZINE EVERY MONTH—STUDY THE *REAL PROS*—THE GREATEST IN ACTION AND EXPRESSION—WHICH IS WHAT CARTOONING IS ALL ABOUT!
LLOYD'S FAVORITE: *JACK DAVIS!*

HERE ARE SOME MORE SAMPLES OF LLOYD'S WORK!

For GM Photographic -
A Chevrolet dealer program.

This stuff was done originally in full, glorious color

A GMC slide film on safety in the
service department - silver medal,
International Film and TV Festival
of New York, 1977

From a Chrysler show on the
troubles facing the industry.

American Motors - a slide show
for an executive sales meeting.

LLOYD WORKS ON TRACING PAPER UNTIL HE GETS IT RIGHT, THEN TO A LIGHTBOX ONTO STRATHMORE. FOR SLIDE ART, HE WORKS ON 100% RAG LAYOUT PAPER, AND THEN USES MAGIC MARKER. HE THEN RUBBER CEMENTS TO 60 # OFF-SET PAPER -THEN CEMENTS TO COLOR-AID BACKGROUND - ON 11 X 14!

PERMISSON FROM LLOYD GOLA

RALPH'S POST

HERE, RALPH, TAKE THIS LETTER BACK! JOE AND I AREN'T SPEAKING!

OKAY, RALPH, GIVE THE LETTER BACK TO ME!

NO, RALPH, TAKE IT BACK! I DON'T WANT THE LETTER!

JAMES H. MALONE

© JAMES H. MALONE

JAMES MALONE

JAMES' METHOD FOR IDEAS VARIES. SINCE HIS SUBJECT IS A POSTMAN, HE'S ALWAYS OBSERVANT WHEN HE GOES TO THE POST OFFICE; HE LOOKS AT PEOPLE AT THE LINE UP... WHAT THEY ARE SAYING, OR NOT SAYING. ALSO THE POSTAL CLERKS, AND THE GENERAL ATMOSPHERE. HE ALSO TALKS TO NEIGHBORS AND MAIL DELIVERERS... THAT TURNS INTO JOKES.

AGE YOU STARTED TO DRAW: FOUR COLLEGE: MOREHOUSE COLLEGE, ATLANTA

ART SCHOOL: CENTER FOR CREATIVE STUDIES, DETROIT PUBLISHED: 30 YEARS

FAR AHEAD YOU WORK: 4-6 WKS AT ONE TIME: 8 LINES AROUND ART: YES

FINAL ART DRAWN ON: MEDIUM BRISTOL ZIP: SOMETIMES WASH: NO

DO YOU USE A LIGHTBOX: SOMETIMES PENCIL GRADE: HB OR B

INK: HIGGINS ERASER: KNEADED BRUSH: 1 OR 2 ONE PANEL: HOUR

PEN POINTS FOR DRAWING: HUNT GLOBE FOR LETTERING: B5½

ADVICE: FIRST, IF YOU'RE IN HIGH SCHOOL OR COLLEGE, SHOW YOUR WORK TO YOUR ART TEACHER AND AFTER THEIR ADVICE FOR IMPROVEMENT, SUBMIT TO YOUR SCHOOL PAPER. IF IT CLICKS THERE, SUBMIT (FOR FREE) TO A NATIONAL PUBLICATION OR SYNDICATE. ACCUMULATE 52 SAMPLES.

© JAMES H. MALONE

METHOD OF WORKING: FIRST I ASSEMBLE ALL THE CARTOON IDEAS THAT I'VE ACCUMULATED OVER THE WEEK, ANALYZE THEM AND CHOOSE THE BEST 8 TO WORK ON. THEN I DRAW LIGHT PENCIL LINES FOR 5"X15" RECTANGLE PANELS ON A LARGE SHEET ON MEDIUM FINISH BRISTOL BOARD. NEXT, WITH A LETTERING GUIDE, I DRAW ABOUT FIVE ROWS OF LINES ACROSS THE UPPER SPACE IN THE PANEL TO ACCOMMODATE 5 LINES OF DIALOG (MY AVERAGE). AFTER BREAKING THE PANEL INTO SMALLER PANELS, I COMPOSE EACH ONE & INK.

THERE'S A LOT OF GOOD CARTOONING HERE. NOTICE HOW JAMES HANDLES HIS GIRL DRAWINGS. HE KNOWS JUST WHAT TO LEAVE OUT... *A REAL PRO*.....GOOD LETTERING TOO. HE HAS DONE EXTENSIVE WORK IN THE FREELANCE MARKETS. SEE NEXT PAGE.

JAMES' CARTOONS HAVE APPEARED IN:

FAYETTEVILLE OBSERVER

ATLANTA PICTORIAL REPORTER

DETROIT FREE PRESS

HEP MAGAZINE

BLACK DIGEST MAGAZINE

ARMY TIMES NEWSPAPER

BROADWAY LAUGHS MAGAZINE

LIGHTHOUSE AND GUIDE MAG.

DETROIT SCHOOLS NEWSPAPER

CHAIN REACTION MAGAZINE

THE DETROIT NEWS

PLAQUEMINES WATCHMAN

HACKETTSTOWN PROSPECTOR

FIRST AUDITION NEWSPAPER

NEWS AND VIEWS NEWSPAPER

SATURDAY EVENING POST

THE ILLUSTRATOR MAGAZINE

NEW YORK AMSTERDAM MAG.

HUMORAMA MAGAZINE

FAMOUS ARTIST MAGAZINE

JACKSON JOURNAL

MICHIGAN CHRONICLE

EBONY MAGAZINE

THE OUTLOOK MAGAZINE

URBAN SCHOOL NEWS

JIVE MAGAZINE

SCHOLASTIC MAGAZINES

ARMY FUN MAGAZINE

SOUL MAGAZINE

SEPIA MAGAZINE

FORWARD NEWS

ARKANSAS JOURNAL

WASHINGTONIAN NEWS

LIBERATOR MAGAZINE

ATLANTIC PICTORIAL REPORTER

BROTHER MAGAZINE

IMPRESARIO MAGAZINE

ATLANTA DAILY WORLD

BLUFFTON NEWSPAPER

ARTISTS IN MICHIGAN

...AND MANY MORE!

MASQUERADE by Ralph Aspinwall

PERMISSON FROM DICKSON-BENNETT, INT. FEATURES

RALPH ASPINWALL

RALPH HAS A GREAT SENSE OF DESIGN IN HIS CARTOONS. HE KNOWS HOW TO GET YOUR EYE TO GO WHERE HE WANTS. HE ALSO KNOWS WHAT TO LEAVE OUT!

RALPH ALSO DRAWS "SUNSET PARK", A STRIP ALSO SYNDICATED BY DICKSON-BENNETT INT. FEATURES.

AGE YOU STARTED TO DRAW: FOUR   HOW LONG PUBLISHED: 14 YRS

COLLEGE: GULF COAST COMM. COLLEGE   DO YOU USE ZIP: YES

ART SCHOOL: ATLANTA ART INST.   FAR AHEAD YOU WORK: 2 MOS.

HOW MANY AT ONE TIME: 4   DO YOU DRAW LINES AROUND ART: YES

FINAL ART ON: 2 PLY BRISTOL   WASH: NO   LIGHTBOX: YES

PENCIL GRADE: 4H   INK: HIGGINS   ERASER: KNEADED

PEN POINTS FOR DRAWING: "BIG SIG" FELT TIP   LETTERING: SAME

BRUSH SIZE: 2   HOW LONG TO DRAW ONE PANEL: 20 MIN-HOUR

WHAT STATE DO YOU LIVE: FLORIDA   HOBBY: GARDENING

DO YOU FREELANCE: 13 YEARS OF FREELANCE BEFORE BECAME SYNDICATED • DO EDITORIAL CARTOON FOR WEEKLY

MASQUERADE by Ralph Aspinwall

ORIGINAL SIZE

METHOD OF WORKING: I USUALLY DO ONE PENCIL ROUGH AND WHEN I'M SATISFIED WITH IT, I PUT IT ON MY LIGHTBOARD AND INK IT ONTO MY PRE-PRINTED "BOX" (PRINTED 50 AT A TIME AT LOCAL COPY CENTER). I PUT THE DATE ON THE PENCIL ROUGH AND KEEP ON FILE. I MAIL THESE CARTOONS TO MY SYNDICATE AT THE END OF THE MONTH!

MORE ABOUT RALPH ASPINWALL....

METHOD FOR GETTING IDEAS: SINCE MASQUERADE IS A COSTUME STRIP, I USUALLY START WITH THE CHARACTER AND THEN JUGGLE PROPS AND SETTINGS UNTIL SOMETHING CLICKS. I THEN WRITE THE GAG ON MY HANDY LEGAL PAD AND LET IT "AGE" FOR A WHILE. THEN, IF I THINK IT'S ANY GOOD, I'LL DRAW IT UP!

ADVICE FOR ASPIRING CARTOONISTS:
PERSEVERE!

MASQUERADE IS A NEW PANEL. "SUNSET PARK" IS MY COMIC STRIP, ALSO SYNDICATED WITH DICKSON-BENNETT. MY FREE LANCE CARTOONS HAVE APPEARED IN MANY NATIONAL MAGAZINES, INCLUDING: GALLERY, CHRISTIAN SCIENCE MONITOR, RED CROSS JOURNAL, HUSTLER, AIR FORCE TIMES, SOLDIER, NATIONAL GUARDSMAN, ARMY TIMES, AND OTHERS. ALSO NUMEROUS TRADE JOURNALS, HOUSE ORGANS, AND ALL GIRLIE MAGAZINES. I ALSO DO A WEEKLY EDITORIAL CARTOON FOR A LOCAL NEWSPAPER. ALSO SERIOUS ILLUSTRATIONS FOR MAGS AND BOOKS. I AM *NOTHING* IF NOT VERSATILE!

"NOBODY PREPARES FOOD LIKE LORETTA, BUT THEY CAME PRETTY CLOSE TO IT IN THE ARMY."

PERMISSION FROM KING FEATURES SYNDICATE, INC.

BILL HOEST

BILL IS A TRULY CONTENTED CARTOONIST... AND TALENTED.

METHOD OF WORKING: *I WORK ALONE, I'M VERY ORGANIZED. I SPEND MANY HOURS AT THE DRAWING BOARD. IT'S LUCKY THAT I LOVE MY WORK.*

METHOD FOR GETTING IDEAS: *OBSERVATION AND THE NEW YORK TIMES. ALSO GAG WRITERS OF EVERY PERSUASION.*

ADVICE FOR GETTING PUBLISHED: *DRAW AS MUCH AS YOU CAN, DEVELOP A STYLE, AND HANG IN THERE.*

AGE YOU STARTED TO DRAW: *THREE* **COLLEGE:** *COOPER UNION*

ART SCHOOL: *NONE* **HOW LONG PUBLISHED:** *15 YEARS* **ZIP:** *NO*

FAR AHEAD YOU WORK: *3 MONTHS* **HOW MANY AT ONE TIME:** *SIX*

LINES AROUND ART: *YES* **FINAL ART ON:** *2 PLY STRATHMORE*

WASH: *ONLY FOR MAGAZINE PANELS* **USE A LIGHTBOX:** *YES*

PENCIL GRADE: *BLUE* **INK:** *INDIA* **ERASER:** *KNEADED*

PEN POINTS FOR DRAWING: *SPEEDBALL AND CROQUIL*

PEN POINTS FOR LETTERING: *SAME* **BRUSH SIZE:** *2 TO 6*

HOW LONG TO DRAW ONE PANEL: *VARIES* **FREELANCE:** *ALSO*

STATE YOU LIVE: *NEW YORK* **HOBBY:** *WOODCARVING*

"NOBODY PREPARES FOOD LIKE LORETTA. BUT THEY CAME PRETTY CLOSE TO IT IN THE ARMY."

ORIGINAL SIZE

PERMISSION FROM KING FEATURES SYNDICATE, INC.

BILL'S ART HAS APPEARED IN: LADIES HOME JOURNAL • GOOD HOUSEKEEPING • PLAYBOY •COSMOPOLITAN • FAMILY CIRCLE • PARADE MAGAZINE: *"LAUGH PARADE"* • BOOKS: ENCYCLOPEDIAS •TEXTBOOKS • THE LOCKHORNS •AGATHA CRUMM •HOWARD HUGE

KEN MUSE

I DON'T REMEMBER WANTING TO BE ANY-
THING BUT A CARTOONIST. I'M LUCKY, THERE
SEEMS TO BE FEW PEOPLE WHO KNOW WHAT
THEY WANT, AND NEVER CHANGE THEIR MIND!
MOST PEOPLE LACK "PASSION" FOR ANY
KIND OF CAREER. I KNOW, BECAUSE FOR
15 YEARS I'VE HAD COLLEGE CLASSES
FILLED WITH THEM.

AGE STARTED TO DRAW: *FIVE* ART SCHOOL: *MEINZINGER, DETROIT*

COLLEGE: *NONE* HOW LONG PUBLISHED: *40 YRS.* FAR AHEAD: *6 WKS*

HOW MANY AT ONE TIME: *12* LINES AROUND ART: *YES* ZIP: *YES*

WASH: *NEVER* LIGHTBOX: *ALWAYS* PENCIL GRADE: *HB, F, H, 2H*

INK: *ARTONE, E.D.* ERASER: *KNEADED* STATE YOU LIVE: *MICHIGAN*

PEN POINTS FOR DRAWING: *1290, 170* FOR LETTERING: *B6, B5½*

HOW LONG TO DRAW ONE: *HOUR* HOBBY: *MUSIC— JAZZ PIANO*

FREELANCE: *YES* SYNDICATE: *NONE*

DON'T LET HER IN, MY HAIR'S A MESS !

ORIGINAL SIZE

© KEN MUSE

HOW I GET IDEAS: I SKETCH-OUT SITUATIONS ON BOND PAPER, WITHOUT ANY END RESULT IN MIND.... THESE SITUATIONS GIVE ME IDEAS FOR GAGS. SINCE THIS STIMULATES THE MIND, IT NEVER FAILS ME !

ADVICE FOR ASPIRING CARTOONISTS: *IF YOU CAN'T "TASTE IT IN YOUR MOUTH".. IF YOU GIVE UP EASY... IF YOU GET DISCOURAGED GETTING REJECTION SLIPS .... IF YOUR FRIENDS AND RELATIVES CAN TALK YOU OUT OF IT... IF YOU CAN'T STOP DRAWING, OR IF IT NEVER ENTERS YOUR MIND YOU'RE NOT GOING TO MAKE IT...* **I WOULDN'T EVEN BOTHER !**

ORIGINAL SIZE

© KEN MUSE

MY METHOD OF WORKING: EVERYTHING IS ROUGHED-OUT FIRST ON BOND PAPER, CLEANED-UP ON TRACING PAPER, AND THEN TRANSFERRED ON 2 PLY STRATHMORE (BOTH MEDIUM AND PLATE FINISH), VIA A LIGHTBOX. THEN INKED. IF YOU'VE EVER LOST ORIGINALS IN THE MAILS, YOU'LL APPRECIATE LIGHTBOXES!

"TEEN SCENE"

PERMISSION FROM DICKSON-BENNETT INT. FEATURES

GODDARD SHERMAN

GODDARD HAS A GREAT STYLE FOR GAG CARTOONS. HE LETS NOTHING GET IN THE WAY OF HIS GAG. HE USES HIS BLACKS EFFECTIVELY AND HAS GOOD LINE WORK!

"DADDY, THIS IS RANDY. HE'S THE ONLY BOY IN SCHOOL WHO'LL EAT THE STUFF I COOK IN HOME Ec."

CARTOONING IS ACTUALLY A HOBBY WITH GODDARD. HIS PROFESSION IS A UNITED METHODIST MINISTER, PASTOR OF A 1200 MEMBER CHURCH IN FT. MYERS, FLA.

AGE YOU STARTED TO DRAW: ELEMENTARY SCHOOL

COLLEGE: BROWN UNIVERSITY   HOW LONG PUBLISHED: 5 YRS.

ART SCHOOL: ART INST. of PITTSBURGH   ZIP: FREQUENTLY

WASH: YES   DO YOU USE LIGHTBOX: YES   PENCIL GRADE: #2

FAR AHEAD YOU WORK: 4-6 WKS.   HOW MANY AT ONE TIME: 12

FINAL ART DRAWN ON: MAG-BOND PAPER-STRIPS-2 PLY BRISTOL

INK: HIGGINS   ERASER: NONE-USE WHITE-OUT   BRUSH: 00,1,2

TO DRAW ONE PANEL: 45 MIN.   STATE YOU LIVE: FLORIDA

PEN POINTS FOR DRAWING: HUNT 513E-CRQQUIL

PEN POINTS FOR LETTERING: SPEEDBALL B6   FREELANCE: YES

ORIGINAL SIZE

METHOD of WORKING: I DRAW A ROUGH IN PENCIL, THEN PLACE IT UNDER THE SAME SIZE PAPER (ON LIGHTBOX) - OR BRISTOL IF IT IS FOR ONE OF MY TWO SYNDICATED STRIPS. I MAKE NOTATION ON THE REVERSE SIDE OF THE PENCIL ROUGH OF EACH MAGAZINE TO WHICH I SEND THE PANEL CARTOON *IF THE ORIGINAL IS LOST, I HAVE ONLY TO RETRACE!*

MORE ABOUT GODDARD SHERMAN....

METHOD FOR GETTING IDEAS: *WRITING A GAG IS LIKE WRITING A STORY: BOTH HAVE PLOT, CAST OF CHARACTERS, ACTION BUILDING TO CLIMAX, ETC. SIMPLY REQUIRES WORK — AND OF COURSE A SENSE OF HUMOR! ALSO, I DO USE QUITE A FEW GAGS FROM SEVERAL GOOD GAG WRITERS, AND I MUST GIVE THEM CREDIT!*

ADVICE FOR ASPIRING CARTOONISTS: *DON'T GET DISCOURAGED. COMPETITION IS KEEN. I KNOW ONE PUBLICATION THAT RECEIVES 1500 CARTOONS A WEEK, AND BUYS FIVE! START AT LESSER ONES, WHERE COMPETITION IS NOT SO STIFF. ABOVE ALL: SLANT PROPERLY.*

GODDARD'S CARTOONS HAVE APPEARED IN:

NATIONAL ENQUIRER · SATURDAY EVENING POST · READER'S DIGEST · GOOD HOUSE-KEEPING · AMERICAN LEGION MAGAZINE · BETTER HOMES & GARDENS · MEDICAL ECONOMICS · SATURDAY REVIEW · BOYS' CHANGING TIMES · NEW WOMAN · SIGN......
AND DOZENS OF OTHERS!

NAME: PAUL GRINGLE **AGE STARTED TO DRAW:** 8 OR 9

COLLEGE: BIARRITZ UNIV., FRANCE - PHOENIX COM. COLL.

ART SCHOOL: SCHOOL OF VISUAL ARTS, ART STUD. LEAGUE

HOW LONG PUBLISHED: ZILLION YEARS **ZIP:** NOT OFTEN

FAR AHEAD YOU WORK: 6 WEEKS **AT ONE TIME:** SIX

LINES AROUND ART: YES **FINAL ART:** 2 PLY KID STRATH.

WASH: HARDLY EVER **LIGHTBOX:** YES **PENCILS:** 2, HB, H

INK: PELIKAN **ERASER:** PINK PEARL **BRUSH:** NO. 2, 3, 7

SYNDICATE: DICKSON-BENNETT INT. FEATURES (COMICS EDITOR)

HOW LONG TO DRAW ONE PANEL: ONE TO FOUR HOURS

HOBBY: TENNIS, PING PONG, FISHING, MUSIC, SKETCHING.

MORE STUFF ABOUT GRINGLE

METHOD OF WORKING

ROUGH IDEAS ON LIGHT BOND OR SCRAP PAPER - DO MANY ROUGHS - THEN REFINE ON LIGHTBOX - TRACE ON THE BRISTOL, INK - ALWAYS DO LETTERING FIRST - EXPERIMENT WITH DIFFERENT TECHNIQUES, TRY DIFFERENT APPROACHES TO SAME GAG - SOMETIMES WILL DEVELOP A WHOLE SERIES OF GAGS FROM ONE BASIC SITUATION - OR IDEA!

METHOD FOR GETTING IDEAS

I GET IDEAS FROM DOING SWITCHES ON OTHER CARTOONS THAT I HAVE IN MY CLIP FILE - NEVER LOOK AT A BLANK PAPER TO GET IDEAS — OR WILL WIND UP WITH AN IDEA FOR A BLANK PIECE OF PAPER - OTHER IDEAS COME FROM LISTENING TO PEOPLE, READING A BOOK, WATCHING OR READING THE NEWS - GOING TO ZOO - PEOPLE WATCHING - ETC, ETC.

ADVICE FOR GETTING PUBLISHED

STUDY THE MASTERS: RUBE GOLDBERG, AL CAPP, SULLIVANT, WEBSTER, MILT CANIFF, ROY CRANE, WALT KELLY, MORT WALKER, DIK BROWNE, SCHULTZ, ETC. - FIND THESE AT YOUR LOCAL LIBRARY, DO ADVERTISING FOR LOCAL BUSINESS PEOPLE, LOCAL PAPERS, TV STATIONS, WORK HARD ON YOUR GAGS - *MORE IMPORTANT THAN DRAWING!* TRY TO GET PUBLISHED, EVEN WITHOUT PAY - VALUABLE EXPERIENCE! TRY A GOOD CORRESPONDENCE COURSE IN CARTOONING.

AS AN EXPERIMENT FOR ONE YEAR,

I CREATED *FOURTEEN* DIFFERENT COMIC FEATURES: *TEN* COMIC STRIPS, AND FOUR PANELS. TWO OF THE STRIPS HAD A SIX WEEK SUPPLY, (36), AND THE REST, A TWO WEEK SUPPLY (12), AND SENT THEM TO THE TEN BIG DAILY SYNDICATES!

THE COMIC STRIPS WERE:

"SUPER SILLY WILLIE"
"CARTOON CHRONICLES"
"DR. BILS"
"OTTO SPACE"
"BEGGER"
"HOWARD"
"RUDY RUDE"
"FAIRVIEW AVE."
"SQUEEGEE"
"ARDITH"

I THINK IT'S EASIER TO GET ON BROADWAY!

THE PANELS WERE:

"AHEAD OF TIME"
"CALORIE CHRONICLES"
"ARDITH"
"DON'T STOP ME"

SORRY

I DID **NOT** SEND ORIGINAL ART!

THE ORIGINALS WERE PHOTOSTATED DOWN TO 43 PICAS (7⅛"), XEROXED, FOLDED, AND INSERTED IN A BUSINESS ENVELOPE. *RETURN POSTAGE IS THE PRICE OF A STAMP!* IF YOU WANT TO REDUCE THE COST EVEN FURTHER, FIND A COPY CENTER THAT CAN GIVE YOU *XEROX REDUCTIONS* AT A SMALL FRACTION THE COST OF PHOTOSTATS!

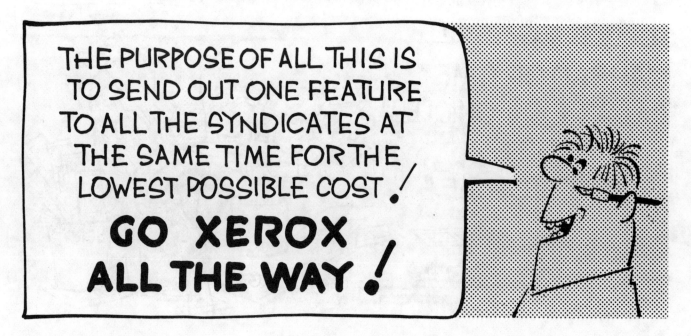

THE PURPOSE OF ALL THIS IS TO SEND OUT ONE FEATURE TO ALL THE SYNDICATES AT THE SAME TIME FOR THE LOWEST POSSIBLE COST! **GO XEROX ALL THE WAY!**

SYNDICATES WOULD RATHER NOT RECEIVE ORIGINAL ART IN THE MAIL

NOT ONLY IS THE COST OF MAILING ORIGINALS EXPENSIVE, BUT *INCONVENIENT!* THE MOST OF WHICH, YOU **CAN'T** IMPROVE THE FEATURE IN ANY WAY... *BECAUSE YOU DON'T HAVE IT!*

THE OTHER DISADVANTAGES:

THEY COULD GET LOST IN THE MAILS

THEY COULD GET MISPLACED AT THE SYNDICATE

A LONG TIME GOES BY BEFORE YOU GET THEM BACK

THE ART COULD GET DAMAGED DURING HANDLING

YOU'LL GET DEPRESSED WHEN THEY COME BACK

YOU'RE ONLY SHOWING ONE SYNDICATE

REMEMBER...YOU'RE GOING TO GET DEPRESSED WAITING WEEKS FOR YOUR ONLY FEATURE TO COME BACK... AND THEN HAVE IT REJECTED! THE SECRET IS TO KEEP BUSY DRAWING NEW FEATURES... AND NEW IDEAS!

HERE'S HOW YOU SEND THEM IN THE MAILS....

GET THEM PHOTO-STATED DOWN TO 43 PICAS (7⅛"), OR EVEN 34½ PICAS (5¾"), WHICH A LOT OF PAPERS ARE RUNNING NOW, AND PUT FOUR TO A PAGE .... THEN XEROX THE WHOLE PAGE ON A STANDARD 8½ X 11 SHEET, AND MAIL THEM IN A BUSINESS ENVELOPE!

MOST SYNDICATES PREFER A
MONTH'S SUPPLY SO THEY CAN
GET A BETTER IDEA IN WHICH
DIRECTION YOUR FEATURE
IS MOVING. YOU CAN ALSO DO
THIS WITH PANEL CARTOONS!

OTTO SPACE

ORIGINAL SIZE

© KEN MUSE

SYNDICATES DON'T WANT A FUNNY SPACE STRIP

YOU'LL GET THESE BACK FROM THE SYNDICATE BEFORE YOU GET HOME FROM THE POST OFFICE. THEY CLAIM THEY ARE FLOODED WITH THIS TYPE OF STRIP. *WHY DON'T THEY WANT THEM?* "THEY'RE NOT WARM AND FRIENDLY, AND THE READER CANNOT RELATE TO THEM!" *WHATEVER THAT MEANS!* I'VE INCLUDED A FEW MORE STRIPS OF "OTTO SPACE" ON THE NEXT PAGE...DON'T WASTE YOUR TIME!

© KEN MUSE

PANELS AND ART DRAWN WITH GILLOTTS 1290-LETTERING : A5½

THIS IS THE OTHER FEATURE, ALSO ONE WITHOUT A CENTRAL CHARACTER. EVERY DAY SOMETHING NEW.

© KEN MUSE

OWING TO THE SUBJECT MATTER.. IT REALLY DOESN'T NEED A CENTRAL CHARACTER. IT'S A SPOOF ON ALL THE PREDICTIONS... CARRIED TO THE RIDICULOUS!!

A FUNNY THING THOUGH, SOME OF THE EARLIER ONES CAME TRUE AND HAD TO BE *REDRAWN*... ONE STEP FURTHER!

THE REASONS FOR REJECTION: "IT WOULDN'T HOLD READER INTEREST". **ANOTHER SAID:** "YOU'LL RUN OUT OF IDEAS". **INTERESTING** COMMENTS AREN'T THEY? YOU COULD PROBABLY TAP EVERY AREA OF HUMAN KNOWLEDGE.... AND WOULD RUN OUT OF IDEAS WHEN YOU DIED!

SOME EXAMPLES OF "AHEAD OF TIME" 50% REDUCTION

BY 1989, NO DECAY, NO CAVITIES, NO DENTISTS!

NO TEETH!

GILLOTTS 1290 FOR DRAWING, AND SPEEDBALL B6 FOR THE LETTERING.

SPEEDBALL A5½ FOR PANEL OUTLINE, AND FOR THE LETTERING.

IN TEN YEARS WE'LL KNOW WHAT POLITICIANS HAVE IN COMMON WITH WORKING PEOPLE!

KEN MUSE

© KEN MUSE

MODERN ART WILL TAKE ITS RIGHTFUL PLACE BEFORE 2017

GILLOTTS 170 FOR DRAWING, SPEEDBALL B5 FOR LETTERING.

1290 FOR ART, B6 FOR LETTERING.

EVERY PERSON WILL HAVE AN I.Q. OF 160 AND OVER!

SINCE THE DISTANCE S IS MADE INFINITE BY COLLIMATING THE INCIDENT BEAM OF LIGHT THE QUALITY $S (\cos 2 + \cos \theta)$ BECOMES INFINITELY LARGE COMPARED...

AT LAST.. PROOF THAT MEN ARE SMARTER THAN WOMEN!

KEN MUSE

B5: LETTERING. B5: FOR THE PANEL OUTLINE.

ORIGINAL SIZE

© KEN MUSE

HERE IS THE COMIC STRIP THAT WAS REJECTED BY ALL THE BIG SYNDICATES FOR LACK OF A CENTRAL CHARACTER. EVERY AREA OF HUMOR WAS USED. IT WAS GREAT FUN TO DRAW BECAUSE I DIDN'T HAVE TO WORRY ABOUT DRAWING THE SAME PERSON OVER AND OVER AGAIN!

HERE ARE MORE SAMPLES OF THE "CARTOON CHRONICLES."

I HAVE A BACHELOR'S DEGREE, A MASTERS, AND A PH.D... AND I STILL CAN'T FIND A JOB!

THAT'S ODD, WHAT'S YOUR DEGREE?

ANCIENT EGYPTIAN DIALECTS, WITH A MINOR IN SANSKRIT!

© KEN MUSE

MY CONTENTION IS THIS: FUNNY THINGS HAPPEN EVERY DAY TO ALL KINDS OF PEOPLE, AND NOT TO ONE PERSON EXCLUSIVELY... ONE DAY IT MIGHT BE THE MILKMAN, ANOTHER DAY, A SCHOOL TEACHER. EVEN THOUGH THIS MAY BE TRUE, IT DOESN'T WORK FOR THE MOVIES. WITHOUT THE CENTRAL CHARACTERS YOU WOULD SOON GET CONFUSED AND QUICKLY LOSE INTEREST. THOSE MOVIES THAT HAVE BEEN WITHOUT CENTRAL CHARACTERS HAVE BEEN DOCUMENTARIES AND COMEDIES. THIS IS WHAT GAVE ME THE IDEA. PEOPLE LOVE STAND-UP COMICS. WHY NOT DO A COMIC STRIP LIKE A STAND-UP COMIC... OR A COMEDY MOVIE?

THE GAGS ARE EASIER TOO IN THIS TYPE OF STRIP. THEY DON'T HAVE TO FIT ONE TYPE OF PERSON. THAT MEANS NO GAGS HAVE TO BE REJECTED AS WOULD BE TRUE OTHERWISE. I PERSONALLY BELIEVE IT TO BE A GOOD CONCEPT, BUT THE SYNDICATES DIDN'T THINK SO!

NOT BEING A PERSON WHO GIVES UP THAT EASY, I WORKED UP ANOTHER IDEA!

CHELOR'S DEGREE, D A PH.D... AND I T FIND A JOB!

ORIGINAL SIZE

© KEN MUSE

DR. BILS

SYNDICATE COMMENTS: ..."TOO SPECIALIZED." ..."FELLOW EDITORS WOULD NOT BUY." ..."NOT A CONCEPT WE FEEL WE CAN SYNDICATE SUCCESSFULLY." ..."A DOCTOR IS TOO NARROW FOR A LEAD ROLL." ..."YOU'LL RUN OUT OF IDEAS." ..."THE AVERAGE READER CANNOT RELATE TO A DOCTOR." ..."THE AVERAGE READER WILL NOT GET DOCTOR JOKES." ..."VERY POOR LEAD CHARACTER. SORRY."

PEN FOR INKING: GILLOTTS 1290. LETTERING WAS WITH A
SPEEDBALL B6. SCREEN WAS FORMATT NO. 7000.

BEGGER

SYNDICATE COMMENTS: ..."I DON'T LIKE ANIMAL STRIPS." .."BEGGER IS NOT STRONG ENOUGH." ..."TOO GROTESQUE." .."SORRY, IT DIDN'T GRAB OUR EDITORS." ..."NOT SUITED TO OUR NEEDS." ..."WE JUST TOOK ON TWO NEW FEATURES." .."I JUST DON'T LIKE IT." ..."ANYTHING ELSE YOU CAN SEND?"

INKED WITH GILLOTTS 1290. LETTERING WAS DONE
WITH A SPEEDBALL B6! FORMATT SCREEN NO. 7000.

DON'T STOP ME

SYNDICATE COMMENTS:..."TOO FAR OUT FOR US". ..."MOST WE DIDN'T GET." ..."I DOUBT THAT EDITORS WOULD BUY IT." ..."SORRY, THIS IS NOT FOR US." ..."WHAT ELSE HAVE YOU GOT?"

I'VE FELT DOWN ALL DAY TODAY!

"DON'T STOP ME" WAS CONCEIVED AS A VERY STRANGE PANEL CARTOON... ON THE WEIRD SIDE! ALL TYPES OF PEN POINTS WERE USED FOR THE PURPOSE OF VARIETY! SOME EVEN I DIDN'T UNDERSTAND!

© KEN MUSE

ARDITH

SYNDICATE COMMENTS: ..."PART OF THE PROBLEM SEEMS TO BE THE GAGS. YOU DRAW WELL, BUT THE JOKES JUST AREN'T FUNNY." ..."ARDITH IS A WARM LITTLE GIRL AND I SUSPECT YOU MAY FIND SOME SYNDICATE TO TAKE THE FEATURE ON." ..."ARDITH IS CUTE BUT I REALLY HAVE RESERVATIONS ABOUT HOW MARKETABLE IT IS." ..."ARDITH HAS A LOT GOING FOR IT, BUT WE'RE OVERLOADED." ..."SORRY AGAIN."

ORIGINAL SIZE

KEN MUSE

© KEN MUSE

CALORIE CHRONICLES

SYNDICATE COMMENTS: ..."SORRY, WITHOUT A CENTRAL CHARACTER I'M NOT INTERESTED." ..."I DOUBT THAT EDITORS WOULD EVEN BE INTERESTED." ..."DOES NOT FIT THE 'FAR SUPERIOR' CATEGORY." ..."I DON'T KNOW WHAT YOU'RE TRYING TO SAY." ..."SORRY."

YOUR PROBLEM IS YOU DON'T GET ENOUGH EXCERCISE!

© KEN MUSE

THOSE YOUNG PEOPLE ARE ALL ALIKE ...
EAT AND RUN!

FOR STARTERS, MRS. BROWN, WE'LL START
YOU ON A LOW CALORIE DIET!

GOOD NEWS, HERB! I'M TAKING YOU OFF WHEAT
GERM AND PUTTING YOU BACK ON VITAMINS!

CALORIE CHRONICLES IS A TAKE-OFF ON HEALTH AND DIET. THE
PANEL WAS OUTLINED WITH A SPEEDBALL B6, AND DRAWN
WITH A GILLOTTS 1290 AND 170. THE LETTERING WAS DONE
WITH A SPEEDBALL A5½. *THE RESPONSE WAS TERRIBLE!*

©KEN MUSE

ORIGINAL SIZE

SQUEEGEE

SYNDICATE COMMENTS: ..."WE ALREADY HAVE TWO PANTOMIME FEATURES." ..."I DON'T LIKE PANTOMIME STRIPS." .."THE CHARACTER IS NOT WARM AND FRIENDLY." .."READERS WILL NOT RELATE TO "SQUEEGEE." ..."YOU'LL RUN OUT OF IDEAS." .."I DOUBT EDITORS WOULD BUY IT." .."THANKS, BUT NO THANKS."

THE SECRET TO A GOOD PANTOMIME STRIP IS USING THE ORDINARY SITUATIONS AND GO ONE STEP FURTHER.... ANOTHER WAY IS TO WORK SITUATIONS *BACKWARDS!*

PEN POINT FOR DRAWING WAS A GILLOTTS 290, AND THE
OUTLINE WAS A SPEEDBALL A5½...*A REAL CHALLENGE!*

ORIGINAL SIZE

HOWARD

SYNDICATE COMMENTS: ..."YOUR MAIN CHARACTER IS RATHER UNSYMPATHETIC". ..."HOWARD IS JUST NOT A WARM ENOUGH CHARACTER". ..."I DON'T FEEL THE IDEA IS GOING ANYWHERE". ..."IT SHOWS A LOT OF PROMISE, BUT WE'RE NOT INTERESTED". ..."VERY PROFESSIONAL, BUT WE'RE BACKED-UP ON FEATURES."

PEN POINT FOR INKING WAS A GILLOTT 1290...ALSO FOR PANEL LINES. LETTERING WAS WITH A SPEEDBALL B6.

© KEN MUSE

RUDY RUDE

SYNDICATE COMMENTS: ..."NOT IN THE 'FAR SUPERIOR' CATEGORY." ..."DOES NOT MEET OUR PRESENT NEEDS". ..."TOO MONSTER LOOKING TO BE ACCEPTED IN A HUMAN CONCEPT". ..."STRONG CHARACTER BUT TOO OBJECTIONABLE AS A LEAD HERO". ..."THE AUDIENCE IT IS AIMED AT IS TOO NARROW". ..."CANNOT BE SYNDICATED."

THIS STRIP WAS DRAWN WITH A GILLOTTS 1290 PEN POINT. THE LETTERING WAS WITH A SPEEDBALL A5½, AND THE PANELS WERE DONE FREEHAND WITH A SPEEDBALL B6!

ORIGINAL SIZE

© KEN MUSE

FAIRVIEW AVE.

SYNDICATE REMARKS: ..."THERE ARE TOO MANY KID STRIPS ON THE MARKET." ..."IT WILL COMPETE WITH OUR OWN KID STRIPS." ..."IT DOES NOT FILL OUR NEEDS AT THIS TIME." ..."I'M NOT AT ALL IMPRESSED." ..."I'M VERY SORRY, BUT I'M JUST NOT INTERESTED." ..."YOUR STRIP IS LACKING IN SOMETHING THAT I CAN'T PUT MY FINGER ON." ..."SORRY, NOT HERE."

I LIKED THIS ONE, BUT I SHOULD HAVE TAKEN MORE TIME TO DEVELOP STRONGER HEROS.

© KEN MUSE

DRAWING PEN POINT WAS A GILLOTTS 1290, AND THE LETTERING WAS WITH A GILLOTTS B6!

THAT'LL BE THE DAY

© KEN MUSE

ORIGINAL SIZE

SYNDICATE COMMENTS: ..."YOU WOULD RAPIDLY RUN OUT OF IDEAS." ..."TOO MONOTONOUS." ..."IT'S A GUT FEELING, BUT I DON'T LIKE IT." ..."I'M NOT INTERESTED IN A COMIC STRIP WITHOUT A CENTRAL CHARACTER." ..."SORRY, BUT THIS SYNDICATE IS NOT INTERESTED." ..."UNUSUAL IDEA, BUT WOULD BE VERY DIFFICULT TO SELL TO EDITORS."

THIS WAS AN EASY STRIP TO DRAW AND A LOT OF FUN THINKING UP IDEAS. THE COMPLETE STRIP WAS DRAWN WITH A GILLOTTS 170 PEN POINT. THE HEAVY STUFF WAS A SPEEDBALL B5!

SYNDICATE REJECTION GLOSSARY

BIGTIME FEATURES

WE ENJOYED LOOKING AT YOUR CARTOONS. UNFORTUNATELY, WE FEEL THEY DO NOT FIT OUR NEEDS AT THIS TIME.

BIGTIME BOB

FUNNY FEATURES

THANKS SO MUCH FOR SENDING ALONG THE SAMPLES OF YOUR COMIC STRIP. I DO NOT BELIEVE, HOWEVER, THAT IT IS SUITED TO OUR NEEDS AT THIS TIME.

MR. I.M. FUNNY

LITTLE FEATURES
SYNDICATE

WE HAVE EVALUATED YOUR SUBMISSION VERY CAREFULLY AND I'M SORRY TO TELL YOU THAT YOUR MATERIAL DOES NOT MEET OUR PRESENT NEEDS. WE WISH YOU BETTER LUCK ELSEWHERE.

MS. FRAN FETURE

OVER THE HILL WORLD-WIDE FEATURES, INC.

YOUR FEATURE IS VERY INTERESTING, BUT IT IS NOT THE SORT OF A FEATURE THAT OUR FELLOW EDITORS WOULD PURCHASE.

BILL MEADOR

THERE'S MORE.....

146

...WE COULD NOT SUCCESSFULLY SYNDICATE YOUR FEATURE AT THIS TIME.

...IT'S LIKELY YOUR FEATURE WAS TOO SIMILAR TO ONE ALREADY ON THE MARKET. EACH SUBMISSION IS EVALUATED BY A TEAM OF QUALIFIED EDITORS.

I HAVE RESERVATIONS ABOUT HOW MARKET-ABLE IT WOULD BE.

...WE ARE OVERLOADED AND DON'T PLAN TAKING ON NEW FEATURES.

...PLEASE KEEP US IN MIND WHEN YOU HAVE ANOTHER IDEA.

...I DON'T SEE ANY REDEEMING QUALITIES IN YOUR COMIC STRIP.

...WITHOUT A CENTRAL CHARACTER..NO!

..THANK YOU FOR THINKING OF US.

...WHILE WE FIND YOUR ART AND HUMOR TO BE GOOD, WE'LL HAVE TO PASS ON THE IDEA. WE DO NOT FIND THE CONCEPT COMPELLING ENOUGH.

...I REGRET YOUR FEATURE DID NOT GET THE SUPPORT NEEDED FOR SYNDICATION.

...THEY ARE NOT SUITED TO OUR PRESENT NEEDS.

...WE HAVE EVALUATED YOUR SUBMISSION AND ARE SORRY TO TELL YOU THAT YOUR MATERIAL DOES NOT MEET OUR NEEDS.

...I'M NOT A FAN OF GIMMICK CARTOON FEATURES...YOUR FEATURE FITS INTO THAT CATEGORY. THERE IS NO GOOD REASON WHY AN EDITOR SHOULD BUY THE FEATURE. I CANNOT HELP BUT BELIEVE YOU'D RUN OUT OF IDEAS WITHIN A YEAR.

I DON'T LIKE SPACE STRIPS

147

REJECTIONS WE'D LOVE TO SEE

WE READ 'EM — WE DON'T GET 'EM!

HAVE YOU INVESTIGATED OTHER AVENUES OF EXPRESSION?

EVERYBODY LAUGHED HERE AT THE SYNDICATE. IT'S THE GREATEST STUFF WE'VE EVER SEEN. A WINNER! UNFORTUNATELY WE ARE TIED UP WITH TWO NEW FEATURES AND LACK THE TIME!

YOU MUST BE KIDDING!

YOUR IDEAS ARE TERRIFIC, BUT YOUR ART WORK IS TOO PROFESSIONAL!

WE WOULD LOVE TO TAKE ON YOUR FEATURE, BUT RAN OUT OF MONEY.

IT'S NOTHING WE CAN PUT OUR FINGER ON, BUT SOME DAY YOU'RE GOING TO MAKE IT... UNFORTUNATELY, NOT WITH US!

TWO REPLIES THAT ARE NEEDED

" I LIKE YOUR IDEAS, BUT YOUR ART WORK IS BAD... CAN YOU GET A CARTOONIST TO DRAW IT FOR YOU?"

"I THINK YOUR CARTOONING IS VERY PROFESSIONAL. CAN YOU GET A PERSON WITH GOOD IDEAS TO WORK WITH YOU?"

SOME CLOSING REMARKS

YOU'RE NOT PAYING YOUR DUES AS A CARTOONIST IF YOU DON'T TAKE PRIDE IN AN *EXTENSIVE* COLLECTION OF REJECTION SLIPS. ALL THE PROFESSIONAL CARTOONISTS WHOSE WORK YOU ADMIRE IN NEWSPAPERS, MAGAZINES, COMIC BOOKS, AND ANIMATED MOVIES, HAVE THEIR REJECTION SLIP COLLECTION. I'M PROUD OF MINE!

AND KEEP THIS IN MIND: IF YOU'RE A FAIRLY GOOD CARTOONIST WITH GOOD IDEAS, DON'T TAKE THOSE REJECTION SLIPS SERIOUSLY. THE SYNDICATES DON'T ALWAYS PICK WINNERS. THERE ARE DOZENS OF TRUE STORIES OF SYNDICATE REJECTIONS OF FAMOUS COMIC STRIPS. ONE SENTENCE FROM A UNIVERSAL PRESS SYNDICATE REJECTION SLIP SAID: "WE WOULD CERTAINLY ENCOURAGE YOU TO SUBMIT YOUR MATERIAL ELSEWHERE, SINCE WE ARE ALL TOO AWARE OF OUR FALLIBILITY."

SO-THIS CHAPTER IS THE RESULT OF AN EXPERIMENT, NOT ONLY TO TEST THE MARKET, BUT THE ATTITUDE OF THE SYNDICATES!

THERE ARE RARE OCCASIONS WHEN YOU WILL RECEIVE A PERSONAL REPLY AND AN HONEST EVALUATION OF YOUR WORK. THE MAJORITY OF REPLIES HOWEVER ARE FORM LETTERS. THAT'S EASY TO UNDERSTAND... HUNDREDS OF ASPIRING CARTOONISTS SEND WORK TO SYNDICATES, AND IF ALL SUBMISSIONS WERE RETURNED WITH A PERSONAL LETTER, THERE WOULD BE NO TIME TO RUN THE SYNDICATE!

BESIDES, THE BULK OF SUBMISSIONS ARE *GARBAGE!*

EVERY SYNDICATE HAS REGRETS OF TURNING DOWN FEATURES THAT LATER BECAME WINNERS WITH ANOTHER SYNDICATE! NO BUSINESS CAN BE 100% RIGHT IN ALL ITS DECISIONS—AND REMEMBER THIS: JUST BECAUSE A FEATURE IS SYNDICATED DOESN'T MEAN IT'S A WINNER—IF THAT WERE TRUE ***NONE WOULD BE DROPPED!***

HERE IS SOME ADVICE FROM EXPERIENCE: SYNDICATES AREN'T INTERESTED IN COMIC STRIPS THAT DO NOT HAVE A CENTRAL CHARACTER!

HOW I LOOKED WHEN I FOUND OUT!

I TRIED UNSUCCESSFULY FOR TWO YEARS WITH TWO FEATURES, ONE A PANEL, THE OTHER, A STRIP! IT MAKES NO DIFFERENCE IF YOUR STUFF IS ORIGINAL, OR THE BEST CARTOONING IN THE WORLD....

DON'T WASTE YOUR TIME.

THERE ARE, HOWEVER, A LOT OF PANELS WITHOUT A CENTRAL CHARACTER. SUCH AS PUZZLES, GAMES, INFORMATION, WEATHER, CONNECTING DOTS, ETC., ETC. THE REASON, I THINK, IS THAT A STRIP WITHOUT A CENTRAL CHARACTER CANNOT BE EXPLOITED IN THE MARKET PLACE FOR TOYS, MOVIES, TV, OR OTHER MARKET-ABLE ITEMS. *WHY NOT... IT IS A BUSINESS YOU KNOW!*

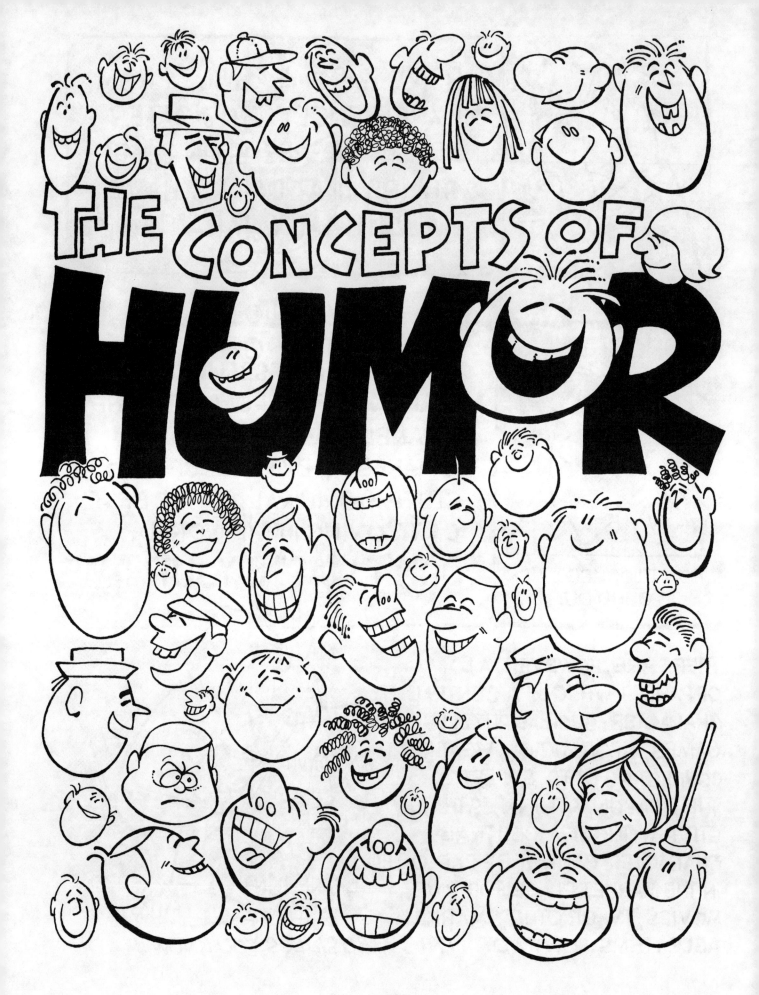

THE CONCEPTS OF HUMOR

HUMOR CAN BE BROKEN DOWN INTO TWO BASICS: "CONCEPTS" AND "CATEGORIES". GAG WRITERS USE "METHODS", "SYSTEMS", AND "CATEGORIES".

THERE ARE NO FORMULAS

WHY ARE THERE NO FORMULAS FOR HUMOR? BECAUSE A FORMULA IS DECLARING SOMETHING DEFINITELY OR AUTHORITATIVELY. YOU CAN'T DO THAT WITH HUMOR! HUMOR IS THE RESULT OF HUMAN FRAILTIES COMING TOGETHER IN THE RIGHT COMBINATION TO PRODUCE A SURPRISE. HUMOR IS SIMPLE TO ANALYZE AFTER THE FACT, BUT ANALYSIS **CANNOT PRODUCE HUMOR!**

HUMOR DOESN'T HAVE TO MAKE SENSE, BE LOGICAL, OR EVEN REASONABLE.

A FUNNY JOKE DOESN'T HAVE TO MAKE SENSE TO BE FUNNY! AS A MATTER OF FACT, IT WOULD BE UNFUNNY THE MORE SENSE IT MADE. WHEN AN ASTRONOMER SEES THE NAMES NEXT TO EACH STAR IN THE NIGHT SKY, WOULD THAT BE REASONABLE?

I DON'T BELIEVE AN ORIGINAL IDEA CAN BE DEVELOPED WITHOUT STARTING WITH NORMAL SITUATIONS!

NORMAL SITUATIONS ARE SOMETHING WE ALL UNDERSTAND! YOUR AUDIENCE CAN RELATE TO THEM, AND YOU USE THAT DEVICE TO TRAP THEM. THEY DON'T SUSPECT WHERE YOU ARE LEADING THEM—*THEN COMES THE SURPRISE!*

SURPRISE IS THE SECRET OF HUMOR! TELL A REALLY FUNNY JOKE TO A PERSON AND NOTICE THE LOOK OF SURPRISE WHEN YOU SPRING THE PUNCH LINE... AND NOTICE HOW THE FUNNY STORIES BEGIN WITH NORMAL SITUATIONS... *OR DIALOG!*

ONE OF THE SYSTEMS, OR **TRICKS** I USE FOR GETTING IDEAS, OR GAGS, WAS TO COLLECT A BATCH OF PANEL CARTOONS AND CUT OFF THE *PUNCH LINES.* THEN LOOK AT THE SITUATIONS FOR GETTING NEW GAGS — LETTING THE DRAWINGS LEAD ME IN A *DIFFERENT* DIRECTION!

OCCASIONALLY, WHEN I GET DESPERATE I RE-ARRANGE THE PUNCH LINES!

IT'S VERY RARE A *TOTAL* GAG WILL POP IN YOUR MIND. THOSE THAT DO ARE ORIGINAL AND ARE ALWAYS THE *BEST*.... IF YOU'RE COUNTING ON THIS HAPPENING FOR ALL YOUR GAGS, THEN I WOULD SUGGEST YOU BECOME A STOCK ANALYST.

YOU'LL SPEND MOST OF YOUR TIME IN THIS BUSINESS SWEATING-OUT THE DEVELOPMENT OF ORIGINAL IDEAS OR GAGS, AND WISHING YOU HAD A NINE TO FIVE JOB!

IF YOU'RE SERIOUS ABOUT CREATING ORIGINAL GAGS, OR IDEAS, SIT YOURSELF DOWN SOME-PLACE WHERE YOU CAN BE ALONE. MUSIC IF YOU LIKE – *NO WORDS!* THEN WRITE DOWN A LOT OF SITUATIONS, LIKE THE ONES BELOW, AND LET THEM STIMULATE YOUR THINKING!

YOU'VE GOT TO START *SOMEWHERE!*

MOB OF PEOPLE ON DESERT ISLAND
VERY THIN MAN ON SCALE
TELEVISION SET ON FIRE
THE DEVIL LEAVING CHURCH WITH 2 BEAUTIFUL GIRLS
GIANT ANT IN DOCTOR'S OFFICE
NEW CAR SHOWROOM ON DESERT
APE LOOKING THROUGH HUGE TELESCOPE

More Situations..

FAT LADY HANGING OVER CLIFF

BABY WATCHING FOOTBALL GAME ON TV

ONE CAT FOLLOWING SIX CATS

PERSON'S HEAD STICKING OUT OF WALL

DESK LOADED WITH TELEPHONES

COMPUTER ON FIRE

BOY ON ROOF OF HOUSE WITH DOG

AMBULANCE PARKED IN FRONT OF X-RATED MOVIE

CAT SITTING ON MAN'S HEAD IN DOCTOR'S OFFICE

GIRL GORILLA ON DESERT ISLAND WITH MAN

AIRPLANE CRASHED IN CLOUDS

DOG AT VETS WITH A MAN ON A LEASH

NAKED MAN STANDING IN UNEMPLOYMENT LINE

UFO IN A NUDIST COLONY

MAN JUMPING HURDLE WITH THREE LEGS

GRASS GROWING INSIDE OF HOME

MUMMY HITCH-HIKING

MATH PROBLEM FILLING ENTIRE BLACKBOARD

ARROW STICKING OUT OF MAN'S CHEST

COMPLICATED INSTRUCTIONS WITH SIMPLE TOY

NOW THAT YOU HAVE ALL THESE SITUATIONS....
WHAT ARE YOU GOING TO DO WITH THEM? YOU
ESSENTIALLY HAVE ONLY **HALF AN IDEA!**

THE OTHER HALF THAT COMPLETES THE GAG IS:

THE PUNCH LINE

PUNCH LINES ARE **CLICHÉS!**

DID YOU KNOW YOU COMMUNICATE WITH PEOPLE
EVERY DAY USING ONLY ABOUT 800 WORDS, AND
IF YOU'RE IN THE SCIENTIFIC OR TECHNICAL FIELD
YOU CAN ADD ANOTHER 400 WORDS?
AND IF YOU LISTEN TO YOURSELF, AND OTHERS
TALK, YOU'LL NOTICE MOST DIALOG IS IN CLICHÉS.

SOME CLICHÉS

"YOU'LL NEVER GUESS WHAT HAPPENED?"

"LET'S GO GET SOMETHING TO EAT."

"SO WHAT HAPPENS NOW?"

"I NEED SOMEONE TO TALK TO."

"HOW MUCH DID THAT SET YOU BACK?"

"WHERE DID YOU PARK?"

"GOT ANY GOOD JOKES TODAY?"

THIS METHOD OF ADDING THE PUNCH LINES TO THE SITUATIONS IS AN OLD AND PRETTY CONSISTENT WAY TO GET USEABLE GAGS, AND SOMETIMES SOME GOOD ONES.

BUT THE REAL MAGIC HERE IS THE MIND'S ABILITY TO SEE, OR DISCOVER GAGS THAT ARE BEYOND THE OBVIOUS ONES THAT RESULT FROM THE RIGHT COMBINATIONS... IN OTHER WORDS, *THE SITUATION AND PUNCH LINE CREATE A NEW GAG!*

IT HAS EVERYTHING TO DO WITH ASSOCIATION AND *NOT* LOGIC!

SOME CRAZY MIXED-UP CLICHÉS

"WHAT DO YOU MEAN I DON'T WORK HERE ANYMORE?"

"I'M WAITING 'TILL IT COMES ON TV."

"THANKS, BUT I DON'T EAT OR DRINK ANYMORE."

"HOW LONG HAVE YOU BEEN WEARING THAT COSTUME?"

"THE LAST TIME I DID THAT I LOST MY JOB."

"NO MATTER WHAT WE DO, THEY STILL WON'T LET US INSIDE."

"NO THANKS, I'D RATHER THROW IT MYSELF."

"I WON'T DO IT, BUT I KNOW SOMEBODY WHO WILL."

"YOU PEOPLE ARE DOING A GREAT JOB HERE!"

"WHEN DOES IT START GETTING FUNNY?"

"I TOLD YOU TO STOP FOLLOWING ME AROUND."

"I WON'T SAY ANYTHING IF YOU WON'T."

MORE WILD CLICHES

"WE'RE ALL OUT OF THAT MODEL!"

"FOR THREE BUCKS I CAN'T COMPLAIN."

"I DIDN'T KNOW ANYONE LIVED THIS FAR OUT."

"BOY, THAT WAS A STEAL FOR $29.95!"

HOW ABOUT THESE:

"IT WAS SUPPOSED TO BE SELF-CLEANING."

"WELL, THERE GOES 5 MILLION BUCKS!"

"I GOTTA GET OUT OF THIS BUSINESS!"

"WE'VE BEEN HAVING LABOR PROBLEMS!"

"WE HAD BETTER CHECK THAT LAST EQUATION."

"I MUST BE DOING SOMETHING RIGHT."

"IT'S OUR NEW FLOOR MODEL!"

"IF IT GIVES YOU ANY TROUBLE, SHUT IT OFF!"

"OPERATOR, OPERATOR, I'VE BEEN CUT OFF!"

"NO, I GOT THIS IN A CAR ACCIDENT."

"OTHER THAN THAT, EVERYTHING'S OK !"

"WHAT DO YOU SEE IN THE FUTURE FOR ME?"

"I THOUGHT THIS WAS GOING TO BE SIMPLE......?"

"HOW MUCH IS THIS GOING TO COST ME?"

"JUST ONCE I'D LIKE TO HAVE THE LAST WORD."

THE BASICS OF HUMOR

THEORETICALLY YOU COULD GO THROUGH THE DICTIONARY AND FIND ALL KINDS OF CATEGORIES FOR HUMOR...

SUCH AS—

FLIRTATIOUSNESS	ABSENT MINDED
WEALTH	FLATTERY
TINKERING	INDIFFERENCE
HAPPINESS	CHILDISHNESS
MIMICRY	DIGNITY
SATIRE	ARROGANCE
FRUGALITY	TEASING
SEX	IRONY
MARRIAGE	CURIOSITY
SNOBBERY	LAZINESS
MEEKNESS	COWARDICE
SARCASM	CLUMSINESS
JEALOUSY	STUBBORNNESS
VANITY	MEDDLING

FOR EXAMPLE – USING CATEGORIES, HUMOR CAN BE CHANNELED!

FLATTERY
FAT LADY TRYING ON DRESS TOO SMALL. SALESPERSON SAYING: "JUST LOOK WHAT THAT DRESS DOES FOR YOUR FIGURE."

ABSENT MINDED
PROFESSOR EXPLAINING MATH FORMULA TO CLASS, THEN FORGETTING HIS HOME PHONE NUMBER.

LAZINESS
MAN CUTTING GRASS THAT'S 10 FEET TALL, COMPLAINING THAT EVERY TIME HE TAKES A NAP, HIS WIFE WANTS HIM TO CUT THE GRASS.

ARROGANCE
CHEMIST USING EXPENSIVE LAB EQUIPMENT TO MAKE COFFEE.

TEASING
LITTLE GIRL WALKING THROUGH DOG SHOW CARRYING A CAT.

CATEGORIES HELP A GREAT DEAL IN COMING UP WITH ORIGINAL IDEAS... IF YOU HAVE ABILITY. *BUT NOT IF YOU DON'T!*

MORE CATEGORIES

CHILDISHNESS
ADULT PLAYING WITH RUBBER DUCK IN BATHTUB.

ANIMALS ACTING HUMAN
WEARING HUMAN CLOTHING, AND TALKING.

INANIMATE OBJECTS
EMOTIONAL INVOLVEMENT WITH MACHINES OR COMPUTERS.

COYNESS
WOMAN PATIENT ASKING IF SHE HAS TO BE EXAMINED ALL OVER AGAIN. DOCTOR SAYING: "NO, JUST YOUR THROAT."

THE TWIST
REVERSING SITUATIONS, OR NORMAL SITUATIONS THAT DON'T GO RIGHT. EXAMPLE: COMPUTER TYPING: "I LOVE YOU."

VANITY
PEACOCK WATCHING ANOTHER PEACOCK, SAYING: "WHAT'S HE GOT THAT I HAVEN'T GOT?"

EXTREME WEALTH
MAN CALLS IRS AND ASKS: "HOW MUCH DO YOU NEED?"

EXAGGERATION
HUGE FAT PERSON STANDING ON SCALE WITH PILE OF CLOTHES NEXT TO SCALE.

DISGUISE
MAN ATTENDING CHURCH IN DEVIL COSTUME — OR MAN IN BEAR SUIT BEING CHASED BY SOME BEARS.

SATIRE
AN EXCELLENT EXAMPLE IS A POLITICAL CARTOON.

STUBBORNNESS
ASTRONAUT PLANTING FLOWERS ON THE MOON.

NEARSIGHTEDNESS
NEARSIGHTED BURGLER WITH GUN TRYING TO HOLD UP OUTSIDE BANKING MACHINE.

PRODIGY
YOUNG CHILDREN SAYING THINGS BEYOND THEIR YEARS. EXAMPLE: BABY ASKING HOW MANY CALORIES IN CANDY.

CLUMSINESS
GROOM KISSING BEST MAN AT WEDDING.

PRETENSE
GUY DRESSED LIKE NAPOLEON AT ARMY RECRUITING.

INDECISION
WOMAN IN SHOE STORE. SHOES PILED 20 FEET HIGH. WOMAN SAYS: "NOW LET ME SEE THE SAME STYLE IN TAN".

CONFUSION
MAN STANDING IN FRONT OF BLOCK OF HOMES THAT ALL LOOK EXACTLY ALIKE.

EMBARRASSMENT
FORGETTING TO REMOVE LENS CAP FROM WEATHER SATELLITE BEFORE IT GOES INTO ORBIT.

OCCUPATIONS
MAKING FUN OF SOME ONE'S JOB. EXAMPLE: PERSON HAS HIS BRAIN REMOVED IN ORDER TO BE A CARTOONIST.

THE CATEGORIES ARE **INTER-RELATED** AND ARE NOT THE BASIS FOR HUMOR. HUMOR IS SIMPLE, AND HAS A NATURAL FLOW. IT IS **SPONTANEOUS**...IT IS NOT CONTRIVED!

IF YOU'RE NOT A FUNNY PERSON BY NATURE... AND I MEAN BY THAT, YOU FIND HUMOR IN EVERYDAY LIFE, YOU WON'T BE SUCCESSFUL SEARCHING OUT HUMOR FOR YOUR CARTOONS OR ANYTHING ELSE, NO MATTER HOW YOU TRY.

HUMOR IS **NOT** LOGICAL!
IT IS EVERYTHING **BUT**!

ARE YOU TRYING TO GET FUNNY WITH ME?

HUMOR IS BEST CREATED, OR DEVELOPED, NOT BY CATEGORIES, BUT BY CONCEPTS!

ALL IDEAS CAN BE DERIVED FROM THE 5 BASIC CONCEPTS:

STUPIDITY
THE OBVIOUS
DECEPTION
THE UNUSUAL
THE RIDICULOUS

STUPIDITY WOULD INCLUDE IGNORANCE, AND THE RIDICULOUS WOULD INCLUDE EXAGGERATION. LET'S CONTINUE WITH EACH CONCEPT AND GIVE SOME EXAMPLES.

STUPIDITY

PEOPLE DO A LOT OF FUNNY THINGS AND SAY A LOT OF FUNNY THINGS FROM STUPIDITY OR IGNORANCE. LIKE A GUY HOSING DOWN HIS MOTOR WHILE HE'S WASHING HIS CAR... OR PUTTING A SALAD IN THE MICROWAVE OVEN. *GAGS ARE EVERYWHERE!*

LIKE THESE:

YOU HAVE TO ADMIT, IT *IS STUPID!*

CONTRAST IS THE SECRET TO **"STUPID HUMOR."**

MORE STUPIDITY IN HUMOR!

© KEN MUSE

THE OBVIOUS

SIMPLY PUT—THE OBVIOUS IS TOO RIDICULOUS TO MENTION. A GOOD EXAMPLE WOULD BE A SOLDIER IN COMBAT, REMARKING TO HIS COMRADE: "A GUY COULD GET KILLED AROUND HERE!" BELOW ARE MORE EXAMPLES TO STIMULATE YOUR IMAGINATION.

WHAT COULD BE MORE OBVIOUS THAN A CRATE OF ARMS?

THE FUNNY THING ABOUT THE OBVIOUS CONCEPT IS THE TOTAL SURPRISE IN STORE FOR THE READER AT THE END!

...ALL BEGINNING NORMALLY!

© KEN MUSE

DECEPTION

DECEPTIVE EXPECTATION IS SAYING.....OR DOING SOMETHING ENTIRELY DIFFERENT FROM WHAT YOU EXPECT FROM THE SURROUNDINGS.... LIKE AN ASTRONAUT ON THE MOON TELLING HIS FELLOW ASTRONAUT HE FORGOT HIS COMB.
SOME MORE EXAMPLES TO STIMULATE YOUR MIND.

A NORMAL SITUATION WITH A DECEPTIVE TWIST!

©KEN MUSE

THE SITUATION IS NORMAL BUT THE COMMENT IS ENTIRELY OUT OF CONTENT... OTHERWISE THE STRIP JUST ISN'T FUNNY!

MORE DECEPTION FROM NORMAL SITUATIONS!

THE UNUSUAL

THE UNUSUAL CAN ALSO INCLUDE THE "WEIRD"! THESE GAGS ARE THE MOST DIFFICULT, AND ALSO THE LEAST UNDERSTOOD. IT WOULD HELP IF YOU HAD A *STRANGE* SENSE OF HUMOR. AN EXAMPLE WOULD BE A MAN WALKING TOWARD MOUNTAINS THAT LOOK LITTLE BECAUSE OF THEIR DISTANCE, AND FINDING THEM AS *LITTLE* AS THEY APPEAR.

LET'S TRY SOME MORE:

A WEIRD ONE... BUT STARTS NORMALLY!

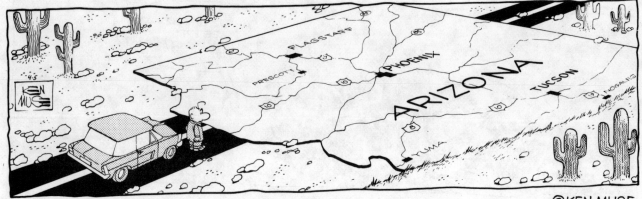

©KEN MUSE

172

THE UNUSUAL ... BEGINNING NORMALLY!

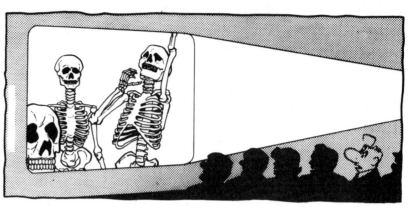

© KEN MUSE

ONCE AGAIN....IF YOU DON'T START YOUR IDEAS WITH THE NORMAL SITUATIONS YOU CAN'T DEVELOP THE GAG!

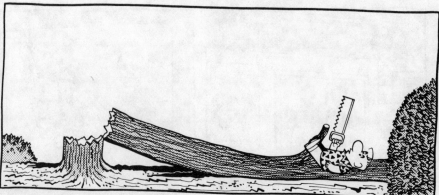

©KEN MUSE

FROM THE UNUSUAL...TO THE WEIRD!

©KEN MUSE

THERE'S NO END TO THE UNUSUAL!

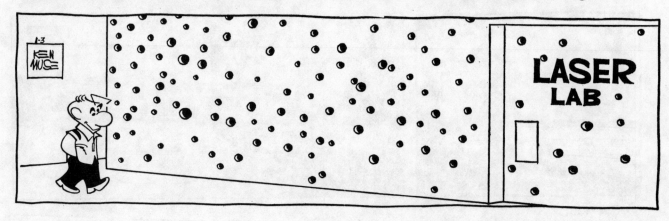

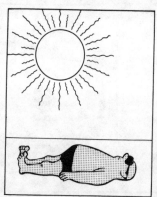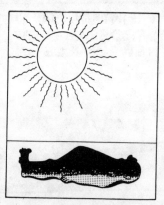

THE RESULT OF MY HEAD INJURY!

KEEP GOING...DON'T STOP NOW!

EVERY SITUATION CAN BE *PUSHED!*

FOR UNUSUAL GAGS YOU'VE GOT TO TAKE YOUR SITUATIONS ONE STEP FURTHER. WORKING BACKWARDS SOMETIMES HELPS!

THE RIDICULOUS

YOU HAVE TO BEGIN WITH THE OBVIOUS AND THEN DISTORT INTO THE RIDICULOUS — FOR EXAMPLE: TWO ARCHAEOLOGISTS IN AN EGYPTIAN TOMB READING HIEROGLYPHICS. ONE SAYS TO THE OTHER: "IT SAYS, "GET OUT OF VIETNAM."

TRY THESE ON:

IT MAY BE RIDICULOUS, BUT IT BEGINS WITH A NORMAL SITUATION!

A CAR FALLING FROM A CLIFF IS A NORMAL SITUATION, HOWEVER UNPLEASANT, BUT A RIDICULOUS COMMENT IS HUMOROUS!

IN THESE SOMEWHAT NORMAL SITUATIONS, THE REMARKS TURN THEM INTO THE RIDICULOUS...THE BEST SOURCE OF GAGS!

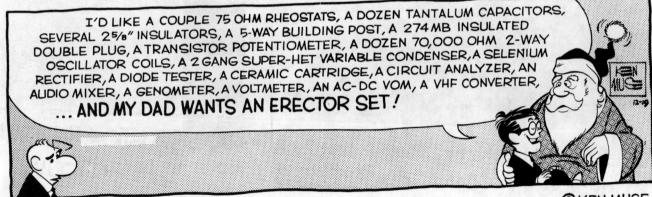

NEITHER THESE FIVE CONCEPTS OF HUMOR NOR ANY THEORY OF HUMOR WILL ENABLE YOU TO CREATE ORIGINAL IDEAS. NOTHING CAN DO THAT..!!
YOU'LL HAVE TO USE YOUR IMAGINATION TO **"SEE INTO"** THESE CONCEPTS.
IT'S VERY MUCH LIKE MUSIC - IF YOU DON'T PRACTICE, YOU'RE NOT INTERESTED.

FOR A TEST OF YOUR SENSE OF HUMOR AND SOMETHING TO **"PUSH"** YOUR IMAGINATION, HERE ARE A SERIES OF GAG PANELS.
ONE IS ALL BLACK ... THE OTHER ALL WHITE, AND OVER EACH IS WRITTEN THE HUMOR CONCEPT!

LIKE THIS:
AND YOU ADD THE PUNCH LINES

THE OBVIOUS

THE OBVIOUS

LIKE THIS:

HEY, FRED, CAN I BORROW YOUR SNOW BLOWER?

JOHN, YOUR GOOD CONDUCT MEDAL IS SCRATCHING ME.!

183

THE OBVIOUS

THE OBVIOUS

THE RIDICULOUS

THE RIDICULOUS

184

THE UNUSUAL

THE UNUSUAL

STUPIDITY

STUPIDITY

DECEPTION

DECEPTION

IT HASN'T BEEN EASY, HAS IT?
THAT'S BECAUSE YOU HAVEN'T PRACTICED!

EVERY CARTOONIST OR GAG MAN WORTH HIS SALT, GOES THROUGH AGONY MOST OF THE TIME CREATING **ORIGINAL GAGS!** THE DIFFERENCE IS THE PRO KEEPS AT IT....!

DECEPTION

SAYING OR DOING SOMETHING ENTIRELY DIFFERENT FROM WHAT YOU EXPECT FROM THE SURROUNDINGS.

DO YOU HAVE THE
MAGAZINE SECTION DEAR?

I THINK MY EYES
ARE GOING, DOCTOR.

THE RIDICULOUS

DISTORTING FROM THE OBVIOUS

YOU'RE A BIG NOTHING, GEORGE.

YOU MADE A WRONG TURN AGAIN.

187

THE OBVIOUS
THINGS TOO RIDICULOUS TO MENTION

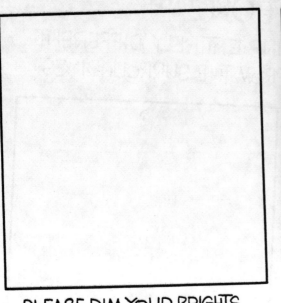

PLEASE DIM YOUR BRIGHTS.

YOU LOOK BETTER IN WHITE DEAR.

THE UNUSUAL
SITUATIONS THAT ARE WEIRD

SO THIS IS THE DEVIL'S TRIANGLE.

I'M WORRIED, THIS IS NOT THE YEAR
FOR A TOTAL ECLIPSE.

STUPIDITY
SELF EXPLANATORY

I THINK THE BULB IS SCREWED IN THE WRONG WAY.

BRACE YOURSELF, WE'RE GOING TO LAND ON THE SUN.

IF YOU REALLY WANT A CHALLENGE, TRY THESE THREE

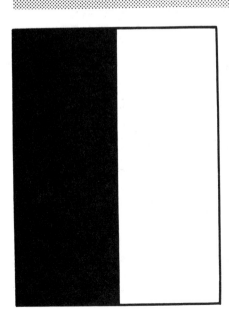  

SOME CLOSING REMARKS ABOUT HUMOR!

I'VE NEVER SEEN OR HEARD A GAG THAT EVERYONE THOUGHT WAS FUNNY!

THE ONES YOU THINK ARE THE FUNNIEST USUALLY GET THE LEAST RESPONSE.

IT'S THE IDEAS THAT SELL, NOT THE ART WORK!

FIND YOUR OWN SYSTEM TO CREATE THE GREATEST NUMBER OF USABLE GAGS

YOU MIGHT CONSIDER BUYING GAGS FROM PROFESSIONAL GAG WRITERS. THERE ARE A LOT OF FUNNY PEOPLE OUT THERE!

DON'T EXPECT TO SIT DOWN AND MAKE UP GREAT GAGS THE FIRST TIME YOU TRY. NO MATTER HOW GREAT THE SYSTEM .... FIRST, YOU GOTTA GET YOUR MIND IN GEAR.

CHECK MY BOOK, "THE SECRETS OF PROFESSIONAL CARTOONING" (PRENTICE-HALL, PG. 288) AND STUDY ALL THE SYSTEMS OF CREATING IDEAS.

DON'T STARE AT BLANK PAPER UNLESS YOU WANT TO EMPTY YOUR MIND.

SUPER CARTOONIST ANSWERS YOUR QUESTIONS!

Q. IF I SOLD A COMIC STRIP, WOULD I HAVE TO QUIT MY STEADY JOB?

A. CAN YOU DRAW WHILE HAVING A NERVOUS BREAKDOWN?

Q. I'M AN ILLUSTRATOR—WOULD THE TRANSITION TO CARTOONING BE A DIFFICULT ONE?

A. NO. IT'S EASIER TO FALL DOWN THAN FALL UP!

Q. IS THERE *ONE* SECRET TO BEING A GOOD CARTOONIST?

A. YES—BUT IF I TOLD YOU, YOU'D TELL SOMEONE ELSE, AND PRETTY SOON EVERYBODY WOULD KNOW!

Q. WHAT KIND OF STRIPS ARE SYNDICATES LOOKING FOR?

A. ONE THAT'S FUNNY TO EVERYONE—WITHOUT PAYING ROYALTIES.

Q. IF I SEND ORIGINAL IDEAS TO THE SYNDICATES
   WON'T THEY STEAL THEM?
A. NO ONE STEALS DAY-OLD NEWSPAPERS.

Q. WOULD PRENTICE-HALL PUBLISH MY BOOK TOO?
A. IT'S UNLIKELY—THEY'RE ALREADY AT THEIR WIT'S-
   END WITH ONE CARTOONIST   —DON'T PUSH IT!

Q. I'VE READ YOUR LAST CARTOONING BOOK.....
A. NOT AS MANY TIMES AS I HAVE!

Q. WHY ARE CARTOONISTS SUCH POOR SPELLERS?
A. THEIR SO BUSY CONCINTRATING ON DRAWING, THEY
   DON'T NOTICE THE POOR SPELING.

Q. IS THERE A WAY TO TELL IF YOU'RE A NATURAL-BORN
   CARTOONIST?
A. THERE SURE IS: WHEN WOMEN LOOK JUST AS
   FUNNY AS MEN DO.

Q. CAN GIRLS BE CARTOONISTS TOO?
A. ONLY THE WELL-ADJUSTED ONES.

Q. WOULD YOU PLEASE DEFINE "ORIGINALITY"?
A. THAT'S EASY— "UNDETECTED IMITATION"

Q. MY WIFE SAYS IF I QUIT MY $100,000 A YEAR JOB TO
BE A CARTOONIST, SHE'LL LEAVE ME. WHAT CAN I DO?
A. I HEARD YOUR QUESTION, BUT WHAT'S THE PROBLEM?

Q. IS THERE *ONE* SECRET TO GETTING GREAT IDEAS?
A. IF I TOLD YOU, YOU'D TELL SOMEONE ELSE, AND
PRETTY SOON EVERYBODY WOULD KNOW.

Q. A BIG SYNDICATE HAS HAD MY COMIC STRIP FOR OVER
THREE YEARS — IS THIS A GOOD SIGN?
A. SURE IS — *GET ONE PRINTED AND PUT A HANDLE ON IT!*

Q. WHY WOULD ANYONE IN THEIR RIGHT MIND WANT TO BECOME
A CARTOONIST?
A. IF YOU DON'T MIND, *I'LL* ANSWER THE QUESTIONS.

Q. JUST WHAT *IS* A CARTOONIST?
A. SOMEONE WHO ORIGINATES OLD JOKES!

Q. HOW DO YOU KNOW WHEN SOMETHING IS FUNNY?
A. WHEN IT HAPPENS TO SOMEONE ELSE.

Q. MY GIRL FRIEND IS A BETTER CARTOONIST THAN
I AM — WHAT CAN I DO?
A. DROP HER — BUT FIRST GET ALL HER CARTOONING BOOKS.

ADVICE

DEVELOP YOUR OWN STYLE.
DRAW ALL THE TIME.
EXPERIMENT WITH PAPER,
PEN POINTS, INK, LETTERING,
TECHNIQUES—

AND
LAUGH
A LOT!

ANIMATION
MARKETS
CARICATURE
COMIC STRIPS
MAGAZINE
FREE LANCE
NEWSPAPER
GAG PANEL

COMMERCIAL CARTOONING

THE FIRST SURPRISE YOU'LL RECEIVE AS A CARTOONIST IS FINDING OUT YOU CAN'T JUST GO OUT AND GET A NINE TO FIVE JOB DRAWING CARTOONS. BUT DON'T LET THAT BOTHER YOU. IT'S NOT BECAUSE THEY DON'T NEED CARTOONISTS. IT'S BECAUSE ADVERTISING AGENCIES AND ART STUDIOS, WHO USE COMMERCIAL CARTOONING, AS A GENERAL RULE, DON'T HAVE ENOUGH CARTOONING WORK GOING THROUGH THE "HOUSE" TO KEEP A FULL-TIME CARTOONIST BUSY ALL DAY. SO MOST CARTOONISTS "FREELANCE" TO THE STUDIO WHO WANTS THEM. IF THERE IS A CARTOONIST THERE ON A FULL-TIME BASIS IT'S BECAUSE HE OR SHE CAN DO OTHER TYPES OF ART- LIKE ILLUSTRATION, RETOUCHING, LAYOUT, LETTERING, ETC.

A PORTFOLIO IS THE WAY TO GET INTO THIS FIELD. YOU SHOULD BE GOOD AT LETTERING AND LAYOUT, AND HAVE A GOOD DESIGN SENSE!

GRAB THE YELLOW PAGES - LOOK UNDER "ART STUDIOS" AND "ADVERTISING AGENCIES". MAKE A PHONE CALL- ASK FOR THE ART DIRECTOR - ASK FOR AN APPOINTMENT — TO SEE YOUR WORK! DON'T JUST BARGE IN! THE ARTIST IS ALWAYS A BUSY PERSON — DON'T SPOIL YOUR CHANCES!

GAG PANELS

NEXT TIME YOU'RE IN A BIG MAGAZINE STORE – GET SOME COPIES OF THOSE JOKE AND GAG MAGAZINES. YOU KNOW – THE KINDS FULL OF GAG PANELS! MOST OF THE CARTOONING IS SO BAD YOU CAN'T BELIEVE IT. BUT THE MAJORITY OF THE GAGS ARE TERRIFIC. THIS IS THE WORLD OF PUNCH LINES – NOT A COLLECTION OF GREAT CARTOONISTS.

YOU DON'T HAVE TO BE A CARTOONIST TO WRITE GOOD GAGS, YOU SHOULD BE A COMPETENT CARTOONIST HOWEVER – IF YOU PLAN TO DRAW THEM. IT'S ONLY FAIR TO SAY, THE GAG MARKET IS A TRAINING GROUND FOR BEGINNERS.

THE SYNDICATED PANELS ARE A DIFFERENT STORY. THE CARTOONING AND GAGS ARE TOP NOTCH!

TO GET INTO THE FIELD YOU'LL NEED TOP NOTCH GAGS AND PRETTY GOOD ART. PICK-UP A "WRITER'S" OR "ARTIST'S" MARKET. THESE WILL GIVE YOU LISTS OF THE MAGAZINES THAT WANT GAG PANELS – AND ARE WILLING TO PAY!

FIRST STUDY WHAT IS SELLING!

CARICATURE

WHEN I WAS A STUDENT IN ART SCHOOL, IT DIDN'T TAKE ME LONG TO DISCOVER THE MONEY MAKING OPPORTUNITIES IN CARICATURE. I'VE DRAWN FOR THE STATE FAIRS, PRIVATE PARTIES, SALES MEETINGS, HIGHSCHOOL ALL NIGHT PARTIES, AND CURRENTLY FOR GRAND OPENINGS AND SHOPPING MALLS. YOU NEED THE ABILITY TO IMMEDIATELY SEE THE DESIGN IN THE FACE... AND WHAT THING IN THE PERSON'S FACE MAKES THEM LOOK LIKE THEY DO. YOU CAN'T AFFORD TO "MISS" TOO OFTEN — OR YOU WON'T BE ASKED AGAIN!

WORKING FAST WITH MAGIC MARKER, PENCIL, CHARCOAL, PASTEL, OR WHATEVER — IS ALL A MATTER OF CONFIDENCE AND PRACTICE!

FOR YOUR PORTFOLIO YOU'LL NEED PHOTOS OF SOME FAMOUS PEOPLE, AND THEN A CARICATURE DRAWING OF THEM TO SHOW WHAT YOU CAN DO. THEY MUST BE INSTANTLY RECOGNIZED! TO GET INTO THE FIELD, TAKE YOUR PORTFOLIO TO HIGH-SCHOOLS, TV STATIONS, BUSINESSES, AND PROMOTIONAL ORGANIZATIONS — AND GET SOME CARDS PRINTED!

FREE LANCE

SINCE THERE AREN'T TOO MANY 9 TO 5 JOBS FOR THE CARTOONIST, IT SORT OF FORCES THEM INTO DOING FREELANCE JOBS. IT SIMPLY MEANS PICKING UP YOUR OWN CARTOONING JOBS — BRINGING THEM HOME, OR TO YOUR STUDIO, AND DOING THEM ON YOUR OWN — AND THEN SENDING THE BILL!

YOUR PORTFOLIO SHOULD CONTAIN CARTOONS AND LOTS OF CARTOON LAYOUTS. ALSO DIFFERENT TECHNIQUES, SUCH AS WATERCOLOR, DESIGNER COLORS, WASH, PEN AND INK, ETC.

YOUR BEST SOURCES FOR FREELANCE ARE: NEWSPAPERS, MAGAZINES, BOOKS, COMIC BOOKS, GAG PANELS, TELEVISION, CARICATURES, ETC., ETC.

YOU GOTTA HAVE A GOOD ATTITUDE!

NEWSPAPERS

NEWSPAPERS HAVE ART DEPARTMENTS, WHERE ALL TYPES OF ART ARE DONE: LAYOUT, KEYLINE, SPOT DRAWINGS, PHOTOGRAPHY, RETOUCHING, AND SOME CARTOONING. THE COMIC STRIPS ARE FURNISHED BY THE SYNDICATES, A FEW BEING DONE LOCALLY!

IF YOU'RE A GOOD CARTOONIST, YOU SHOULD TRY SOME OF THE LOCAL WEEKLY PAPERS IN YOUR AREA......OFTEN THEY ARE LOOKING FOR BEGINNING EDITORIAL ARTISTS. TWO OF MY EX-CARTOONING STUDENTS ARE DOING JUST THAT.

PHONE FOR AN APPOINTMENT WITH THE ART DIRECTOR AND TAKE IN SOME OF YOUR BEST SAMPLES. REMEMBER— YOUR LINES SHOULD BE ABLE TO TAKE AT LEAST A 50% REDUCTION— DRAWING "ACTUAL SIZE" IS A RARITY!

DON'T TRY THE BIG DAILIES FIRST— IF YOU DON'T GET HIRED YOU'LL GET DISCOURAGED. WORK THE WEEKLIES AND GET YOUR STUFF IN PRINT!

DON'T EXPECT TO MAKE BIG BUCKS RIGHT AWAY. YOUR TALENT WILL GET BETTER AND BETTER — AND THAT'S LIKE HAVING MONEY IN THE BANK!

POLITICAL CARTOONING

ARE YOU A PERCEPTIVE CARTOONIST? ARE YOU KNOWLEDGEABLE ABOUT CURRENT EVENTS? CAN YOU COMMUNICATE WITHOUT WORDS IN YOUR CARTOONS? ARE YOU A **VERSATILE** CARTOONIST? IT'S A BIG ORDER ISN'T IT? YOU BET IT IS!

MOST EDITORIAL CARTOONING BORDERS ON *ILLUSTRATION*. ILLUSTRATION IS *REALISTIC ART*, BUT EDITORIAL CARTOONING IS A MIXTURE OF *BOTH*. NO SIMPLE FEAT!

THE WAY TO GET INTO THE BUSINESS, IF YOU THINK YOU'RE QUALIFIED, IS TO VISIT YOUR LOCAL PAPERS, BOTH LARGE AND SMALL. SHOW THE MANAGING EDITOR YOUR WORK. REMEMBER— A GOOD CARTOONIST WITH GOOD EDITORIAL IDEAS WILL NOT BE TURNED AWAY TO DRAW FOR A RIVAL NEWSPAPER. THAT'S NOT GOOD BUSINESS. BUT YOUR WORK HAS TO BE CONSISTENTLY EXCELLENT! GOOD LUCK!

ANIMATION

THIS IS A TOUGH FIELD TO GET "ON THE JOB TRAINING" IF YOU DON'T LIVE IN AN AREA WHERE ANIMATION IS BEING PRODUCED. BUT THOSE ARE THE BREAKS!

IF YOU LIVE IN SUCH AN AREA, YOU MAY NOT EVEN KNOW IT. CHECK THE YELLOW PAGES UNDER "ANIMATION", AND TAKE OVER YOUR SAMPLES. BUT REMEMBER — IF YOU HAVE NO IDEA HOW ANIMATION IS DONE, OR NOT EVEN TRIED TO FIND OUT, AND EXPERIMENTED ON YOUR OWN, THEN NO ONE IN THE BUSINESS IS GOING TO BE INTERESTED.

THEY ARE LOOKING FOR GOOD CARTOONISTS THAT HAVE A BURNING DESIRE TO ANIMATE! NO LESS!

THERE ARE SCHOOLS THAT TEACH CARTOONING AND ANIMATION. LOOK IN THE AD SECTION OF "AMERICAN ARTIST" MAGAZINE!

ANIMATION IS COMPOSED OF KEY DRAWINGS OF ACTION WITH DRAWINGS DONE INBETWEEN, BY "INBETWEENERS". THEN THE PENCIL DRAWINGS ARE TRACED ON CELS BY INKERS. THEN COLORED ON THE REVERSE SIDE BY THE "OPAQUERS". COMPUTER ANIMATION IS THE THING NOW — BUT YOU STILL NEED AN "ANIMATOR" TO PROGRAM THE THING.

THIS IS THE ONLY ART FIELD I KNOW WHERE YOU CAN HAVE GOOD ART AND GOOD IDEAS AND DRAW YOUR BRAINS OUT — AND STILL GET NOWHERE!

WHY? PROBABLY BECAUSE THE SYNDICATES DON'T REALLY KNOW WHAT THEY'RE LOOKING FOR—UNTIL THEY SEE IT! SORT OF LIKE SELLING POPULAR SONGS!

THERE'S ONE FACT: "YOU HAVE TO WANT TO DRAW A COMIC STRIP SO BAD THAT YOU CAN TASTE IT IN YOUR MOUTH — AND REFUSE TO GIVE UP."

THE ONLY ADVICE I CAN GIVE IS DON'T TRY WITH JUST "ONE" COMIC STRIP. DRAW SEVERAL IDEAS AND KEEP THEM IN THE MAIL CONSTANTLY. AT LEAST THEY'LL KNOW WHO YOU ARE!

ONE THING ABOUT STRIPS—YOU DON'T *REALLY* HAVE TO BE A GOOD CARTOONIST—BUT YOU NEED A GOOD CONCEPT! A NEW APPROACH! A NEW WAY OF SAYING SOMETHING! A PERSONALITY!

BE PREPARED FOR TONS OF REJECTION SLIPS—AND A FEW PERSONAL LETTERS. YOU'LL NEVER FIGURE IT OUT!

TELEVISION

THIS IS A RAPIDLY CHANGING ART FIELD WHERE COMPUTERS SEEM TO BE TAKING OVER THE JOBS OF ARTISTS. THIS IS PARTIALLY TRUE!

AT ONE TIME, *TELEVISION* WAS A MECCA FOR ALL KINDS OF ARTISTS. THE ART DEPARTMENTS ARE STILL INVOLVED IN NEWSPAPER, TRADE, AND TV GUIDE ADS. ALSO ON THE AIR PROMOTION, SLIDES, PHOTOGRAPHY, KEYLINE — AND SOME CARTOONING. THE BEST ADVICE FOR THOSE CARTOONISTS WHO WOULD LIKE TELEVISION — HOP DOWN TO ALL OF YOUR LOCAL STATIONS AND SHOW THE ART DIRECTOR YOUR CARTOONS!

THERE IS ALSO MUCH SET DESIGNING IN THE ART DEPARTMENT. TELEVISION ARTISTS ARE A WELL-ROUNDED AND MANY TALENTED PEOPLE.

TELEVISION IS NOT THE PLACE FOR THOSE WHO CAN ONLY DRAW CARTOONS — ONLY FREELANCE!

GREETING CARDS

THEY PREFER THAT ARTISTS AND CARTOONISTS LIVE IN THE AREA. GREETING CARD ARTISTS DO EVERYTHING. THERE ARE DEPARTMENTS OF LETTERING, LAYOUT, WRITING, OIL PAINTING, WATERCOLOR, POETRY, CARTOONING, ETC. THIS IS WHERE YOU'LL FIND TOP-NOTCH CARTOONISTS AND GAG WRITERS. MANY SYNDICATED CARTOONISTS GOT THEIR START IN THIS BUSINESS. EXPERIMENTATION IS THE NAME OF THEIR GAME.

WHERE ARE THE COMPANIES? THAT'S EASY— LOOK ON THE BACK OF THE GREETING CARDS!

WANT TO GET IN THE BUSINESS? YOU GOTTA BE GOOD! WRITE OR PHONE FOR AN APPOINTMENT. BRING IN YOUR PORTFOLIO. HAVE CARTOONING, LETTERING, IDEAS, ETC.

NO ONE'S GOING TO TURN AWAY A GOOD ARTIST!

MAGAZINES

CHANCES ARE GOOD THAT SOME SORT OF MAGAZINE IS PRINTED IN YOUR AREA. PROBABLY MORE THAN YOU IMAGINE. EACH ONE HAS AN ART DIRECTOR AND A SMALL STAFF AND CONTRIBUTING ARTISTS AND WRITERS – AND GAG PANELS – AND SPOTS!

HEAD FOR YOUR MAGAZINE STAND. GET THE NAME AND PHONE NUMBER OF THE ART DIRECTOR! ... IF YOU CAN DO OTHER ART JOBS THAT'LL BETTER YOUR CHANCES. IF YOU DON'T TRY, YOU'LL NEVER KNOW.

GET A COPY OF **WRITER'S MARKET** YOU'LL GO INTO SHOCK WHEN YOU DISCOVER HOW MANY MAGAZINES ARE PUBLISHED IN THIS COUNTRY – AND ALL OF THEM DEPEND ON ARTISTS, WRITERS, AND PHOTOGRAPHERS. IT BOGGLES THE MIND – IT BOGGLES MY MIND!

THE *YELLOW* PAGES WILL LIST ALL THE LOCAL MAGAZINES PUBLISHED IN YOUR AREA!

THERE'S CARTOONING OUT THERE!

JUST ABOUT EVERY PROFESSION HAS ITS *INSIDE* PUBLICATIONS, WITH CARTOONISTS AND GAG WRITERS BEING NO EXCEPTION. NO ONE OF THEM IS BEST. EACH ONE SERVES UP SPECIAL INFORMATION ABOUT NEW MARKETS, OLD MARKETS, RATES, AND VARIOUS BREAKDOWNS OF MARKETS INTO GAGS AND STYLES. I'VE INCLUDED ONE THAT COVERS ABOUT ALL THE INFORMATION YOU'LL NEED TO ENTER THE BUSINESS... *GOOD LUCK AND HAVE FUN!*

THE GAG RECAP
P.O. BOX 86 EAST MEADOW, N.Y. 11554

Enclosed is a sample copy of THE GAG RECAP. This fine publication, now in its 29th year, gives a thorough coverage of the major and middle-class cartoon markets each month.

Most of the top names in the cartoon business are subscribers. They find THE GAG RECAP a valuable aid in checking the originality of gags, address of markets in need of material, prices paid for cartoons, and appropriate slants for specific magazines. It is also a reference as to when and where a certain cartoon has been published. Our back editorial pages cover informative current news.

Editors use it to check the originality and quality of cartoons submitted to them. Cartoonists find out if gagwriter material is fresh. They see what type of cartoon each editor prefers and also use it as a check for pay-on-publication magazines that may need their memories jogged before paying off. Gagwriters are also able to weed out stale ideas before submitting them. The GAG RECAP is a constant thought-stimulator, providing a never-ending source of gag bases.

For the cartoonist who does not use gagwriters, tHE RECAP is like having the best writers in the country working for you. The ideas of all the top men are here for you to use. There is no end to the number of saleable ideas that a nimble mind can come up with merely by making legitimate switches on the gags found in THE GAG RECAP.

May we help You with YOUR gags?   Sincerely,   Al Gottlieb,
                                                 Editor & Publisher

CONTENTS OF THE GAG RECAP

MAY 1983

GENERALS	PAGE	RATE	NO.	X-RATED	PAGE	RATE	NO.
				CAVALIER	8	50	17
AM.LEGION	3	50	2	EASYRIDERS	8	35	12
B H & G	3	300	2	GENT	9	25	7
BOYS LIFE	3	75	6	**GENTLEMANS COMPANION	9	?	16
CHANGING TIMES	3	250	3	HARVEY	9	25	12
CHICAGO	3	100	7	IRON HORSE	10	35	17
COSMO	3	225	6	PENTHOUSE	10	300	16
DYNAMIC YEARS	3	25	3	PLAYBOY	10	350	24
EBONY	3	50	4	PLAYGIRL	11	125	6
FAM.CIRCLE	4	250	2				
FIELD & STREAM	4	100	2	WEEKLIES-			
GD HSKPING	4	200	9	NAT.ENQUIRER	11,18	210	39
L H J	4	200	1	NEW YORKER	12,18	$600	89
LION	4	30	1	REVIEW OF NEWS	14	25	10
MODERN MATURITY	4	35	--	STAR	14,19	45	14
NAT.LAMPOON	4	50?	8	T V GUIDE	15	125	1
NEW WOMAN	4	50	25	WOMANS WORLD	15	100	26
OMNI	5	150	14				
READERS DIGEST	6	125	10	DAILIES			
ROTARIAN	6	50	4	KING FEATURES	16	35	26
SAT.EVE.POST	6	125	29	McNAUGHT SYNDICATE	17	25	10
V F W	7	25	4	WALL ST.JRNL.	17	65	20
WOMAN	7	10	30				

EDITORIALS---p. 19,20

** New Addition to GAG RECAP coverage.

NOTICE THE CONTENTS OF THE RECAP MAGAZINE
AND HOW ALL THE MARKETS ARE COVERED.
THIS TERRIFIC PUBLICATION WILL KEEP YOU BUSY!
SEND FIVE DOLLARS FOR A SAMPLE COPY.
HERE ARE THE RATES:
THREE MONTHS (3 ISSUES) $12.00
SIX MONTHS (6 ISSUES) $22.00
ONE YEAR (12 ISSUES) $40.00

GENERAL MAGAZINES

AMERICAN LEGION(M)(MAR)700 N.Pennsylvania St, Box 1055 Indianapolis IN 46206 $50
(Harbaugh) TV newscaster:"...two extraterrestrials were picked up today at a downtown
         video game arcade posing as instructors.. ."
(Maul)   Driver to cop:"Why don't you people get organized! One day you take away my
         license and now the very next day you ask to see it!"

BETTER HOMES & GARDENS(M)(APR)Dan Kaercher,1716 Locust St.,DesMoines IA 50336 $300
(Maul)   Man to waitress:"Hi! Welcome to our table. My name's Stan and with me tonight
         is my partner in life, Liz. We'll be your customers for this evening..."
(Harbaugh) IRS agent to bum:"First off, let me congratulate you for having four children
         in college..."

BOYS LIFE(M)(APR)Joseph Connelly,1325 Walnut Hill La, Irving TX 75062 $75
(Busino) Rabbit with touching ears:"When I do this with my ears, I can pick up UHF TV
         signals."
(Carpenter) Vet to dragon:"Nothing serious, your pilot light just went out is all."
(Wayne) Vet with periscope, to giraffe;"Say aahhhh."
(Brown) Rabbit to waitress; "A bacon, lettuce and tomato on rye."
(Busino) Cat stays dry by walking under dog's belly in rain.
(Flynn) Kangaroo filling pouch with water:"He wants a waterbed!"

CHANGING TIMES(M)(APR)Ellen Roberts,1729 H St NW, Wash. DC 20006 $250
(Harbaugh) Sign at IRS:"E=mc^2--Evasion Equals Comeuppance to the Max Squared"
(Lepper) Host in empty house:"Then I said to him, so sue me!"
(Martin) Sign on front lawn:"Garage Sale--Men's Wear, Teen Shop, Gift Boutique, etc"

CHICAGO(M)(APR)A.H.Kelson,3 Illinois Center,303 E Wacker Dr, Chicago IL 60601 $100
(Vey)   Fish at bar, to man:"Why? Do I look like a fish?"
(Cullum) Dutchman selling man wooden shoes:"They're made in Italy."
(Schwadron) Chairman to board:"Heads, we go global; tails, we liquidate"
(")   Voice from General Motors penthouse:"Cocaine! Why didn't we think of that?"
(Cheney) Sign at IRS:"Thank You for Not Whimpering"
(")   Gal to date in wrecked restaurant:"Does champagne always make you burp like that?"
(")   Orchestra conductor near car on stage:"May I have your attention,please? Would
         the owner of the vehicle bearing plate number 946-VHB..."

COSMOPOLITAN(M)(APR)Stephen Whitty,224 W 57 St NY,NY 10019 $225
(Martin) Gal peeling flower petals:"He loves me, he loves his frumpy bootish middle-
         aged wife..."
(Cotham) Gal to guy on floor:"Jeffrey, do you realize we just had our first quarrel?"
(Gerberg) Sexy clerk to boss at clock shop:"Mr Davidson! Please! Let your second hand
         sweep someplace else!"
(Mirachi) Fortune teller to dame:"In a 'menage a trois' you will be number 'trois'"
(Shirvanian) Guy to gal in gym:"I don't mind you earning more money than I do or driving
         a more expensive car, but dammit, Janice, do you have to bench press more than I
         do too?"
(Power)Gal to date:"I don't get it. You're not married, you don't have herpes, I'm having
         a great time...what's the catch?"

DYNAMIC YEARS(BM)(APR)H Pryor,215 Long Beach Blvd, Long Beach CA 90801 $25
(Schochet) Wife as they leave party:"Stop snickering. I tell you he was after my body!"
(")   IRS agent to payer;"I see you've deducted your Liars Club dues."
(")   Clerk re: book on sale:"Overcoming Procrastination":"Ten people said they'd be
         in to buy it tommorrow."

EBONY(M)(APR)Stella Evans,820 S.Michigan Ave Chicago IL 60605 $50 (Black characters)
(Machamer) Housewife to plumber in diving suit:"How bad is it?"
(-)   Boss to applicant with sandwich sign:"You are very lucky,Mr. Jones. WE DO have
         an opening in our advertising department."   ...
...

CARTOONING BOOKS

WHEN I WAS A KID I ATE AND BREATHED CARTOONING. I BOUGHT EVERY CARTOONING BOOK I COULD GET MY HANDS ON – THE LIBRARY WASN'T GOOD ENOUGH – I HAD TO OWN THEM SO I COULD STUDY THEM CONSTANTLY – I STILL DO!

YOU GET SOMETHING FROM EVERY BOOK —

HERE'S A LIST OF CARTOONING BOOKS, MOST OF THEM I HAVE. I'VE READ THEM ALL – THEY'RE GREAT – *EVEN MINE!*

THE WORLD ENCYCLOPEDIA OF COMICS

MAURICE HORN

CHELSEA HOUSE PUB. NEW YORK   1976

THE COMICS

COULTON WAUGH

MACMILLAN, NEW YORK · 1947

ANYTHING YOU CAN GET YOUR HANDS ON

MORE GREAT CARTOONING BOOKS

COMIC ART
AND
CARICATURE

ROY PAUL NELSON

CONTEMPORY BOOKS, INC.
CHICAGO · 1978

CARTOONING

ROY PAUL NELSON

CONTEMPORY BOOKS, INC.
CHICAGO

FELL'S GUIDE TO
THE ART OF
CARTOONING

ROY PAUL NELSON

CONTEMPORY BOOKS, INC.
CHICAGO

THE
COMPLETE
BOOK OF
CARTOONING

JOHN ADKINS
RICHARDSON

PRENTICE-HALL

LEARNING
TO
CARTOON

SID HOFF

STRAVON EDUCATIONAL PRESS

TOP CARTOONISTS
TELL HOW THEY
CREATE AMERICA'S
FAVORITE COMICS

ALLEN WILLETTE

ALLIED PUBLICATIONS, INC.
FLORIDA · 1964

THE ART
OF
CARTOONING

JACK
SIDEBOTHAM

M. GRUMBACHER, INC.,
460 WEST 34 ST. NY. 10001

HOW TO
DRAW COMICS
THE
MARVEL WAY

STAN LEE AND
JOHN BUSCEMA

SIMON & SCHUSTER, NY. 1973

CARTOONING
THE HEAD
AND FIGURE

JACK HAMM

GROSSET AND DUNLAP
NEW YORK · 1978

– AND STILL MORE

DRAWING AND SELLING CARTOONS

JACK MARKOW

GROSSET AND DUNLAP
NEW YORK · 1964

DRAWING COMIC STRIPS

JACK MARKOW

GROSSET AND DUNLAP
NEW YORK · 1972

CARTOONISTS AND GAG WRITER'S HANDBOOK

JACK MARKOW

WRITER'S DIGEST BOOKS
CINCINNATI, OHIO · 1979

I CAN DRAW COMICS AND CARTOONS

FRANK C. SMITH

SIMON AND SCHUSTER
NEW YORK · 1982

THE LEXICON OF COMICANA

MORT WALKER

COMICANA, INC. 1980
MUSEUM OF CARTOON ART
COMLY AVENUE
PORT CHESTER, NY. 10573

YOU CAN DRAW CARTOONS

LOU DARVAS

DOUBLEDAY AND CO.
GARDEN CITY, NY. 1960

THE ART OF HUMOROUS ILLUSTRATION

NICK MEGLIN

WATSON-GUPTILL PUBLICATIONS, NY.
PITMAN PUBLISHING, LONDON · 1973

THE SECRETS OF PROFESSIONAL CARTOONING

KEN MUSE

PRENTICE-HALL, INC.
ENGLEWOOD CLIFFS, N.J. 1981

CARTOONING IN THE USA

ROY WILSON

CHESHIRE PRODUCTIONS · 1974
BOX 494, TORRINGTON, CT. 06790

—WE'RE STILL GOING

CARTOONING

GEORGE F. HORN

DAVIS PUBLICATIONS, INC.
WORCESTER, MASS. 1965

GRAPHIC HUMOR

STAN FRAYDAS

REINHOLD PUBLISHING CORP.
NEW YORK · 1961

THE ART OF THE COMIC STRIP

GRAPHIS PRESS
8001 ZURICH,
SWITZERLAND · 1972

WOMEN IN THE COMICS

MAURICE HORN

CHELSEA HOUSE PUB. 1977
70 WEST 40 ST. NY. 10018

INTRODUCTION TO CARTOONING

RICHARD TAYLOR

WATSON-GUPTILL PUBLICATIONS
NEW YORK · 1947

CARTOONERAMA
CARTOON COURSE

LEO STOUTSENBERGER

BOX 263
BRANFORD, CT. 06405

TIPS FROM TOP CARTOONISTS

DON ARR CHRISTENSEN

DONNAR PUBLICATIONS
21790 YBARRA ROAD
WOODLAND HILLS, CA. 91364

THE COMPLETE GUIDE TO CARTOONING

GENE BYRNES

GROSSET & DUNLAP
NEW YORK · 1950

COMIC ART IN AMERICA

STEPHEN BECKER, SI

SIMON & SCHUSTER
NEW YORK · 1959

OTHER BOOKS, TOO, ARE GREAT FOR YOUR REFERENCE WHEN DRAWING CARTOONS — HERE ARE A FEW I THINK ARE GREAT!

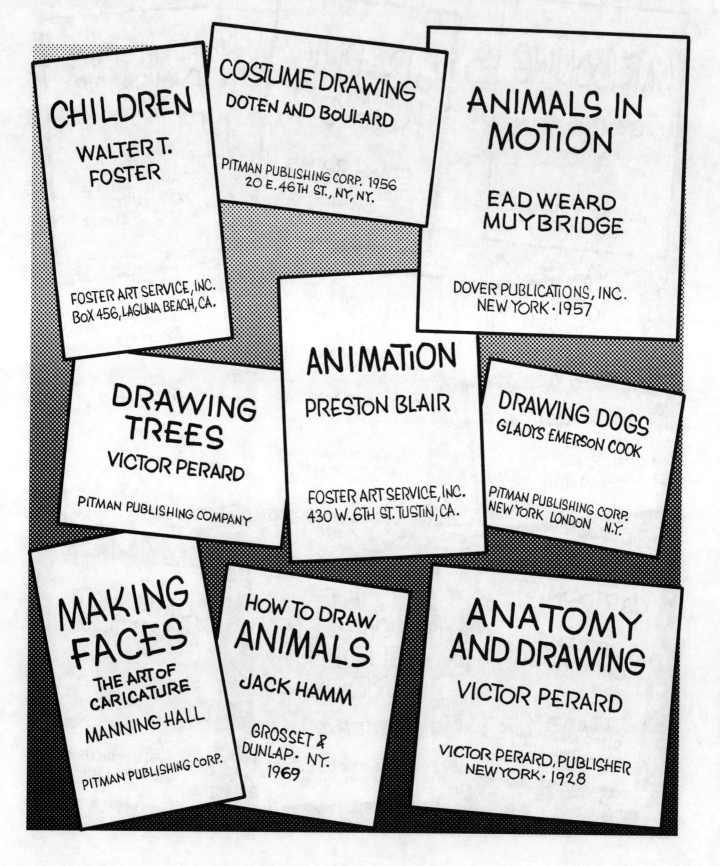

CHILDREN
WALTER T. FOSTER

FOSTER ART SERVICE, INC.
BOX 456, LAGUNA BEACH, CA.

COSTUME DRAWING
DOTEN AND BOULARD

PITMAN PUBLISHING CORP. 1956
20 E. 46TH ST., NY, NY.

ANIMALS IN MOTION

EADWEARD MUYBRIDGE

DOVER PUBLICATIONS, INC.
NEW YORK · 1957

DRAWING TREES
VICTOR PERARD

PITMAN PUBLISHING COMPANY

ANIMATION
PRESTON BLAIR

FOSTER ART SERVICE, INC.
430 W. 6TH ST. TUSTIN, CA.

DRAWING DOGS
GLADYS EMERSON COOK

PITMAN PUBLISHING CORP.
NEW YORK LONDON N.Y.

MAKING FACES
THE ART OF CARICATURE
MANNING HALL

PITMAN PUBLISHING CORP.

HOW TO DRAW ANIMALS
JACK HAMM

GROSSET & DUNLAP · N.Y.
1969

ANATOMY AND DRAWING
VICTOR PERARD

VICTOR PERARD, PUBLISHER
NEW YORK · 1928

EVEN THOUGH "CARTOONERAMA" WAS COVERED EXTENSIVELY IN "THE SECRETS OF PROFESSIONAL CARTOONING", I'LL BRIEFLY OUTLINE THE COURSE - AND SHOW SOME PLATES!

LEO STOUTSENBERGER'S "CARTOONERAMA" CORRESPONDENCE CARTOONING COURSE IS, I THINK, THE BEST OF ITS KIND AVAILABLE TODAY. LEO, PERSONALLY DIRECTS AND CORRECTS THE STUDENT'S WORK ON TRACING PAPER - RIGHT OVER THE ORIGINAL. IT WOULD BE HARD TO FIND ANYONE THAT IS MORE CONSCIENTIOUS!

WRITE TO: "CARTOONERAMA" BOX 263, BRANFORD CT. ZIP IS 06405!

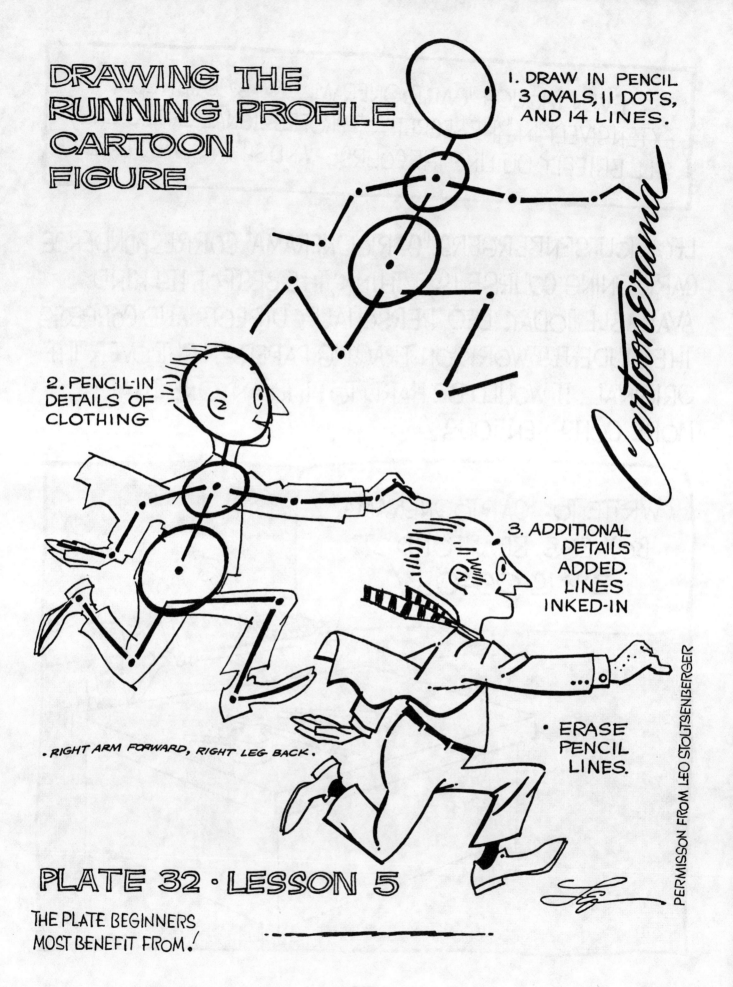

DRAWING THE RUNNING PROFILE CARTOON FIGURE

1. DRAW IN PENCIL 3 OVALS, 11 DOTS, AND 14 LINES.

2. PENCIL-IN DETAILS OF CLOTHING

3. ADDITIONAL DETAILS ADDED. LINES INKED-IN

· ERASE PENCIL LINES.

· RIGHT ARM FORWARD, RIGHT LEG BACK ·

CartoonErama

PERMISSON FROM LEO STOUTSENBERGER

PLATE 32 · LESSON 5

THE PLATE BEGINNERS MOST BENEFIT FROM !

216

Techniques, Tricks and Textures

Cartoonerama   PLATE 37   · LESSON 16

THE FIRST "CARTOONERAMA" PLATE BY LEO STOUTSENBER, WAY BACK IN 1956

WRITE TO:

"CARTOONERAMA"
BOX 263, BRANFORD, CT.
06405

Crammed with never before published information, the book is shown here about one third its actual size. A whopping 330 pages of how to draw cartoons with a dazzling cover printed in many vivid colors.

THE SECRETS OF PROFESSIONAL CARTOONING

KEN MUSE

PRENTICE-HALL

THIS IS A BOOK EVERY ASPIRING CARTOONIST SHOULD HAVE

THE SECRETS OF PROFESSIONAL CARTOONING has been in the book stores for a short time but already has broken all publishing records for books on the subject. Ken Muse, the author has been a professional cartoonist for many years. He's scored great success with his own widely syndicated comic strip, and was a cartoonist animator for various studios. His work as a television art director and author of two books dealing with every conceivable aspect of the photographic arts make him a unique and highly versatile cartoonist-author.

Why are we promoting Ken's book with such enthusiasm when our main concern should be with giving you all the pertinent information possible about Cartoonerama? Because we know that if you buy Ken's book ($11.95 in soft cover) you will be convinced that, although Ken's is the best book on the subject of cartooning, Cartoonerama is the finest course on the subject available today. It's as simple as that.

PERMISSION FROM LEO STOUTSENBERGER

I MENTIONED THE "ARTIST'S MARKET" IN MY LAST CARTOONING BOOK — NOW I'M DOING IT AGAIN BECAUSE IT'S AN AMAZING BOOK FOR ALL TYPES OF COMMERCIAL ART, INCLUDING 8 PAGES OF CARTOONING MARKETS! THE COST IS ABOUT $14.95. WRITER'S DIGEST BOOKS IN CINCINNATI, OHIO PUTS IT OUT. THEY ARE PUBLISHED EVERY YEAR. DON'T BE WITHOUT ONE!

CONTENTS: INTRODUCTION · **USING YOUR ARTIST'S MARKET** · SELF PROMOTION · PRICING YOUR WORK · ADVERTISING, **AUDIOVISUAL & PUBLIC RELATIONS FIRMS** · ARCHITECTURAL, INTERIOR & LANDSCAPE DESIGN · ART/DESIGN STUDIOS · **BOOK PUBLISHERS** · BUSINESSES · GREETING CARDS & PAPER PRODUCTS · MAGAZINES · **NEWSPAPERS & NEWSLETTERS** · PERFORMING ARTS · RECORD COMPANIES · SYNDICATES AND CLIP ART FIRMS · **FREELANCING** · CONTRACTS · *AND MUCH MORE!*

ADDITIONAL INFORMATION

GOOD CARTOONING MEANS NOT ADDING TOO MUCH TO THE DRAWING

NOBODY BECOMES A CARTOONIST BECAUSE SOMEONE SUGGESTED IT - THEY WERE BORN THAT WAY. DRAWING CARTOONS IS REWARD ENOUGH

A GOOD INKER CAN MAKE A POOR DRAWING LOOK GREAT - A POOR INKER CAN MAKE A GREAT DRAWING LOOK BAD!

BUY THE BEST DRAWING CHAIR YOU CAN FIND

CARTOONS ARE READ JUST LIKE WORDS - KEEP IT SIMPLE

DON'T SCREW YOURSELF UP DRAWING ONLY WITH MAGIC MARKERS - LEARN THE PEN AND BRUSH FIRST

WORKING ALL THE TIME WITH FLUORESCENT LIGHTING IS BAD FOR YOUR EYES. USE ORDINARY LIGHT BULBS IF POSSIBLE.

MORE ADDITIONAL INFORMATION

USE YOUR MORGUE - OR CLIP FILE
EVERYTIME YOU DRAW

MAKE YOUR POINT IN A GAG AS SOON AS POSSIBLE

NEVER BLOW A GOOD JOB WITH POOR LETTERING

A CIRCLE WORKS BETTER THAN AN OVAL FOR KIDS' HEADS

DON'T BE AFRAID TO INNOVATE

DON'T WORRY ABOUT TECHNIQUE -
IT WILL DEVELOP

EXAGGERATE PERSPECTIVE

FINDING THE RIGHT TOOLS IS HALF THE FUN!

GET A GOOD ANATOMY BOOK

BEING DIFFERENT LASTS ONLY AWHILE

START WITH ROUGH SKETCHES FIRST

IF YOUR RELATIVES AND FRIENDS DON'T
LOOK FUNNY TO YOU - YOU'RE NOT A CARTOONIST

THE FUNNIEST THINGS ARE SAID
BY PEOPLE WHO AREN'T FUNNY

THE WAY YOU DRAW HANDS IS A DEAD GIVE AWAY TO YOUR CARTOONING ABILITY

MORE ADDITIONAL ADDITIONAL INFO

BUY A BUNCH OF DIFFERENT PEN POINTS –
INK WITH ALL OF THEM UNTIL YOU FIND YOURS

INK ON EVERY SURFACE YOU CAN FIND
UNTIL YOU FIND YOUR FAVORITE

DRAW WHAT IS THE MOST DIFFICULT FOR YOU
15 MINUTES EVERY DAY

FIND SOMETHING FUNNY IN EVERYTHING

FIND A GOOD GAG PANEL – DRAW THE SAME
SITUATION IN YOUR STYLE – THEN ADD YOUR OWN GAG

MAKE FRIENDS WITH OTHER CARTOONISTS –
YOU NEED EACH OTHER

CREATE AT LEAST ONE ORIGINAL GAG EVERY DAY

NEVER LET A DAY GO BY WITHOUT DRAWING

ALWAYS BE PREPARED WITH A
PORTFOLIO OF YOUR CARTOONS

TO BE A CARTOONIST –
YOU HAVE TO THINK LIKE A CARTOONIST

*REMEMBER – IN CARTOONING
EVERYTHING GOES*

SUNDAY COMIC PAGE LAYOUT

THIS IS A 1/2 PAGE STANDARD SUNDAY COMIC PAGE!

SIZE IS 12⅝ X 18½, AND THE NAME OF THE FEATURE IS PUT IN THE FIRST PANEL. YOU DON'T SEE MANY OF THESE FORMATS AROUND.

THIS IS THE TABLOID FORMAT COMIC PAGE

THIS IS SIMPLY DONE BY TAKING OUT PANEL TWO AND STACKING UP THE PANELS IN FOUR TIERS. THERE ARE A LOT OF THESE FORMATS IN THE SUNDAY FUNNIES!

WOW WOW WOW WOW WOW WOW WOW WOW WOW

NAME OF STRIP HERE

THIS IS THE 1/3 PAGE STANDARD FORMAT!

TO GET THE STRIP TO 1/3 PAGE THE TOP ROW OF PANELS ARE REMOVED. *A LOT OF THESE!*

EDITORIAL

LOOK ABOUT YOU. WE'RE IN THE AGE OF MEDIOCRITY. IT'S NO LONGER NECESSARY TO LEARN YOUR CRAFT. JUST DO YOUR *THING!* AS A RESULT OF ALL THIS, THE PROFESSIONAL GETS AS MUCH RESPECT AS THE AMATEUR - THE AMATEUR MAYBE MORE.

I PERSONALLY HAVE STRONG FEELINGS ABOUT THOSE ENTERING ANY PROFESSION UNQUALIFIED. IF THERE'S NO DESIRE TO PUT FORTH EFFORT IN DEVELOPING THE CRAFT - WHATEVER IT IS - THEN A LESS DEMANDING OCCUPATION SHOULD BE INVESTIGATED.

ALL PROFESSIONALS ON TOP OF THEIR FIELD HAVE A DRIVING PASSION THAT NEVER SUBSIDES. IT'S JUST SOMETHING THEY CAN'T CONTROL. THIS PASSION ISN'T *PICKED UP* ALL OF A SUDDEN, IN YOUR 20'S OR 30'S, IT'S BEEN AROUND FOR AS LONG AS YOU CAN REMEMBER.

RESPECTING THE IDEAS IS **FOREMOST**... BUT I NEVER BOW DOWN TO THEM. A POOR DRAWING CAN JUST AS EASILY DESTROY A GOOD IDEA, AND IF THE PUBLIC ISN'T EXPOSED TO GOOD CRAFTSMANSHIP - HOW WILL THEY EVER KNOW?

THE INDEX

INDEX

INDEX

INDEX